Birth of a Dream Weaver

Also by Ngũgĩ wa Thiong'o

FICTION

Wizard of the Crow
Petals of Blood
Weep Not, Child
The River Between
A Grain of Wheat
Devil on the Cross
Matigari

SHORT STORIES

Secret Lives

PLAYS

The Black Hermit
This Time Tomorrow
The Trial of Dedan Kimathi (with Micere Mugo)
I Will Marry When I Want (with Ngũgĩ wa Mĩriĩ)

MEMOIRS

Detained: A Writer's Prison Diary
Dreams in a Time of War: A Childhood Memoir
In the House of the Interpreter: A Memoir

ESSAYS

Globalectics
Something Torn and New
Decolonising the Mind
Penpoints, Gunpoints, and Dreams
Moving the Centre
Writers in Politics
Homecoming

Birth of a
Dream Weaver

A WRITER'S AWAKENING

Ngũgĩ wa Thiong'o

Harvill *Secker*
LONDON

3 5 7 9 10 8 6 4

Harvill Secker, an imprint of Vintage,
20 Vauxhall Bridge Road,
London SW1V 2SA

Harvill Secker is part of the Penguin Random House group of companies whose
addresses can be found at global.penguinrandomhouse.com

Penguin
Random House
UK

First published by Harvill Secker in 2016

penguin.co.uk/vintage

A CIP catalogue record for this book is available from the British Library

ISBN 9781846559891

Printed and bound in Great Britain by Clays Ltd, St Ives PLC

Penguin Random House is committed to a sustainable future for our business,
our readers and our planet. This book is made from Forest Stewardship Council®
certified paper.

MIX
Paper from
responsible sources
FSC® C018179

In memory of Minneh Nyambura, now reborn in her grandchildren of the same name: Nyambura wa Mūkoma, Nyambura Sade Sallinen, and Nyambura wa Ndūcū. Her spirit also lives on in her other grandchildren: June Wanjikū, Chris Ng'ang'a, and Ngũgĩ Biko Kimunga.

Contents

Note on Nomenclature

In this memoir the armed resistance the British dubbed Mau Mau is called by its rightful name, Land and Freedom Army (LFA). Their fighters will be called soldiers.

Prologue

I entered Makerere University College in July 1959, subject of a British Crown Colony, and left in March 1964, citizen of an independent African state. Between subject and citizen, a writer was born. This is the story of how the herdsboy, child laborer, and high school dreamer in *Dreams in a Time of War* and *In the House of the Interpreter* became a weaver of dreams.

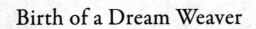

Birth of a Dream Weaver

Sir Bunsen with the Queen Mother at Makerere graduation,
February 20, 1959

1

The Wound in the Heart

"A British officer cannot do a thing like that. That's why . . .
"Why what?"
"A British officer. That's why. That's all."

Queen's Court, where I leaned against a pillar trying to make sense of the news, was named in honor of Queen Elizabeth after she and the Duke of Edinburgh visited Uganda in April 1954. The court, a rectangle enclosed by buildings and fronted by Grecian pillars, was the center of the arts complex, which housed, among others, the English Department. My fellow students Bahadur Tejani, Bethuel Kurutu, Selina Coelho, and Rhoda Kayanja passed me by, gesturing me to join them, but I ignored their overture. Would they feel my woes?

Peter Nazareth might have understood. Though a year ahead of me in college, he was actually the younger by two years; he was born in Kampala, Uganda, in 1940 and I in Limuru, Kenya, in 1938. We had worked together for *Penpoint*, the literary magazine of the Department of English, but he had just graduated, having passed the editorship on to me. So I communed with myself, alone, trying to rally my nerves in a reality I felt helpless to alter. My one-act play, *The Wound in the Heart*, would not be allowed at the Kampala National Theater in the annual nationwide drama festival.

We lived in different halls of residence, a life fraught with friendly rivalries in arenas ranging from sports to drama, and every winning play in the interhall English competition on the Hill had always been re-presented at the only major theater in town. Having the drama appear on a national stage was the most coveted outcome of a win. It carried no material reward, a little reminiscent of the drama on the Greek acropolis of old,[1] where the recognition of a fictive creation surpassed any material gain.

The previous year, 1961, *The Rebels*, my first ever one-act play, another Northcote Hall entrant, had placed second to the winner, Nazareth's *Brave New Cosmos*, a Mitchell Hall entrant that subsequently saw light on the Kampala stage. Nazareth, at the time of his *Cosmos*, had already blossomed into the All-Makerere personality, a presence in music, sports, theater, student politics, and writing.[2] I had lost the final accolade to an icon on the Hill, but I had not given up. And this year, 1962, my play *The Wound in the Heart* had won. My story "The Village Priest" garnered the prize in the short-fiction category, and the two had helped Northcote Hall win the entire competition. Hugh Dinwiddy, the hall warden, hailed the overall outcome as exciting news, "because the quality of the work done in order to win it was very good"[3] and also because "so many members of the hall had offered their services towards this end." My stars were well aligned. *On to the National Theater we go*, I thought.

I sensed that something was wrong when, as time passed, the intense buzz surrounding the National Theater appearance fizzled out. The professors who I thought would know were evasive, but eventually I cornered David John Cook.

Cook was one of the two faculty members most active in support of students' artistic endeavors. A graduate of Birkbeck College, University of London, Cook had visited Makerere from the University of Southampton briefly in 1961 and then came back in 1962 with tenure. He threw his youthful weight behind the already growing local talent, those who came after the earlier generation of David Rubadiri, Erisa Kironde, and Rebecca Njau, who had been mentored by Margaret MacPherson, the spirit behind the emergence of the first generation of student writers on the Hill and the proud founding member of the English Department in 1948.[4]

The department was the crown jewel of a college started in 1922 as a technical high school that became a degree-awarding institution, affiliated with the University of London, in 1949. MacPherson has chronicled this story in the book *They Built for the Future*,[5] the title derived from the Makerere motto. The college served the entire British East and Central African empire, taking students from mainly Uganda, Kenya, Tanganyika, Zanzibar, Malawi (then Nyasaland), Zambia, and Zimbabwe (then Northern and Southern Rhodesia). The English Department was the house of the language of power in the colony.

I found Cook in his department offices. He had supported my efforts and was one of the first to congratulate me on the win. He was friends with John Butler, poet and headmaster of Lubiri Secondary, a leading high school in Kampala, who was a regular presence in both the Uganda Drama and Student Drama festivals and was the one who had adjudicated the competition that my play had won. Cook invited me to sit down, but he did not seem enthused to see me. I went straight to the point: Did he know why the play was denied the stage at the National Theater?

Not looking directly at me, he said something about the British Council, race relations, and all that. And then the words. "They don't think a British officer can do that." He became uncharacteristically busy, shuffling the papers on the table. "They have nothing against the play as a play," he mumbled, "but they think a British officer could not do that!"

The play is set in Kenya during the armed liberation struggle against the British settler state. Mau Mau was the name the British had given to the liberation movement, otherwise known as the Land and Freedom Army, which started fighting the colonial state in 1952. The British sent many of its soldiers and civilian supporters to concentration camps, then deceptively called detention camps. *The Wound in the Heart* is built around an LFA (Mau Mau) soldier who returns home from such a concentration camp, only to find that a white district officer had raped his wife. The rape is not acted out; it's mentioned, narrated rather than shown. The main thread in the theme is not the rape but the man's initial refusal to come to terms with change.

John Butler, the adjudicator, described the play as being beautifully written and finely constructed and praised the production and the players for living up to the quality of the play.[6] And because Butler was a member of the drama festival committee, he must have been an advocate for the play's inclusion. Was he outvoted, overruled even, all because it was inconceivable that a British officer could have forced himself on an African woman? The art of politics by some who did not like the politics in the play had trumped the art of drama.

Cook was just the messenger of bad news, not the perpetrator, but as I stood in Queen's Court, his words continued, repeating in my mind like a broken record: *a British officer cannot . . .* Eventually, I walked away and turned left toward the Main Building, not sure if I should go to the Library or back to my hall of residence. The Main Building, a replica of the main building of the University College, London, housed the offices of the principal, the registrar, and their underlings. It was the multipurpose center of Makerere political and administrative life; major assemblies were held here; its floor became a dancing arena on weekends, a display of moves and formal attire, often organized by the popular MABADA, acronym for Makerere Ballroom Dancing Association. Located at the highest point on the Hill, the Main Building was a cross-center for students and faculty and visitors from any point of the campus.

I bumped into Ganesh Bagchi and his wife Sudharshana. They taught at Government Indian Secondary School, Old Kampala, which opened in 1954. They were an inseparable couple. They did a lot of performances together, some of them Bagchi's own sketches. With Erisa Kironde, a black Ugandan, the Indian couple were the most prominent on a cultural scene otherwise largely dominated by the expatriate white community.

Being in theater, Bagchi and Sudharshana seemed the prefect recipients of my woes. They had lived long enough in colonial Uganda, and I wondered whether, as Indian writers in the racially divided Kampala literati, they had had experiences similar to rejection of a play on account of its content.

My listeners shook their heads in a gesture of helpless sympathy.

I went back to my room, number 75 on the second floor, lay on my bed, a cacophony of sounds around the refrain *"a British officer . . . that's why . . . that's all"* played in my mind, leading to the same question: a British officer cannot do that, really?

Absurd it seems?
Sometimes we ask questions
Not for answers we don't have
But for the answers we already have.

2

A Wounded Land

I

Images of the numerous atrocities committed by the white settler regime in Kenya compete within me. It is not so much
the wanton massacres, the mass incarcerations, and the violent
mass relocations; these were too large to take in wholly at the
time. It's the singular, the apparently errant, and the bizarre
that creep to mind.

It is Molo. A white settler lends his white visitor a horse to
ride to the station, seventeen miles away. He orders a worker,
probably the one who looks after the stable, to walk with the
rider so he can bring the animal back. The iron-hoofed horse
trots; the barefoot worker runs to keep pace. On the way back,
the tired worker mounts the horse. Whites who see a black
body on a horse report the sacrilege.

The settler owner flogs the worker. European neighbors
come to watch the sport. As evening descends, the exhausted
master ties the worker with a rein and locks him up in a storehouse. After a sumptuous evening meal, the master goes back
to the storehouse, finds the worker lying unconscious, the rein
loosened a little. The master is concerned less with the uncon-

scious condition than the loose chain. It's a sign of attempted escape. He ties the captive tighter than before, fastens the man's hands to a post, and locks the door. Master sleeps well; the worker sleeps forever. This takes place on June 10, 1923.

When eventually the case reaches the courts held in the Nakuru Railways Institute before Justice Sheridan, the outcome rests on the intention, not of the killer, but of the murdered. Apparently before he passed out, he had been heard to say, "I am dead." The all-white jury reached a unanimous verdict: the torture had nothing to do with his death. He had willed it. Natives did not die under settlers' hands; they willed their death. The jury finds the settler guilty only of grievous hurt. The *East African Standard* of August 2–10, 1923, covered the case extensively, and clearly, judging from her archives, Karen Blixen drew from the coverage in her retelling of the story in her memoir, *Out of Africa*.[1] She knew the settler's real name, Jasper Abraham, but interestingly, never mentions it.

Though the way she tells Kitosch's story, the clarity of the details in particular, would suggest that the case disturbed her, Blixen, who writes as Isak Dinesen, ends up not denouncing the travesty of justice but seeing, in the death of the native, "a beauty all its own." In his will to die is "embodied the fugitiveness of the wild things who are, in the hour of need, conscious of a refuge somewhere in existence; who go when they like; of whom we can never get hold."[2] Death from torture becomes a thing of beauty. It's the way of the wild, a mystery, at which a rational mind can only marvel.

How easily the zoological image flows out of the liberal and conservative pens of white travelers in Africa. In 1909 Theodore Roosevelt in his safari to East Africa was awed by the wild man and wild beast reminiscent of Europe twelve thousand years before. The Dane and the American looked through the same race-tinted glasses. Earlier in the book, she had said that what she learned from the game of the country was useful to her in her dealings with the native people.

Blixen's world straddled Kenya as a British company property and as a Crown Colony, 1920 being the demarcation year. Baroness Blixen left Kenya in 1931 for her Danish homeland. But when in 1952 the "Mau Mau" war for land and freedom broke out and Governor Evelyn Baring declared a state of emergency, the scene and the wish to die theory reappeared on a larger stage, the whole country. Its reappearance had a history to it.

A year into the war (or the Emergency, as it was called), the government hired Doctor J.C. Carothers, MB, DPM, author of *The African Mind and Disease*,[3] and paid the psychiatrist handsomely to study "Mau Mau." In 1955 this expert on the African mind published the results under the title *The Psychology of Mau Mau*.[4] He diagnosed Mau Mau as mass mania manifesting itself in violence and witchcraft.

He was not original. In 1851, a hundred years before him, Samuel A. Cartwright, another self-avowed expert on the black mind, this time in the USA, had presented a paper, "Diseases and Peculiarities of the Negro Race,"[5] to the Louisiana Medical Association, diagnosing the desire to escape slavery as a mental disorder, which he gave the name drapetomania. A severe seizure of the mania resulted in the victim's actually attempting to run away from the slave heaven.

Carothers's medical science and Cartwright's before him tapped into a mix of the mythic and Christian: witches, witchcraft, and devil possession. The settler, like his historical slaver counterpart, saw his system as natural, rational, laudable, God's goodness manifest; its defiance, a deviation and departure from the desirable norm, a devil's manifesto. Now, hired medical science sided with his profitable but warped view of the universe. In Cartwright, the union of psychiatry, psychology, and Christianity found its apotheosis in a slave plantation; in Carothers, in a settler colony. Cartwright's cure, amputation of the toes, making it impossible to get far on foot, is echoed in Carothers's call for amputation of the soul, making it impossible to desire freedom. Both recommended prevention by casting out the devil that made them carry out crazy ideas: in Cartwright's case, by continuous torture to induce permanent submission; in Carothers's, by quarantine of thousands into concentration camps and by forced confession of their sins. But the most highly recommended cure by the two experts was the imperative: make them work. Work cleanses. In Kenya, the recommendations move from the desk of a psychologist to that of Evelyn Baring, former governor of Southern Rhodesia 1942–1944, appointed governor of Kenya in 1952. The doctrine becomes official: "Once a man can be led to the position of having to do some work and so purge himself of the Mau Mau oath he has taken, there is a chance that he will be rehabilitated."[6]

There's a problem. The afflicted don't want to be freed of their affliction. They are political prisoners, not slaves, they say. But to their British captors, *captive* rhymes with *slave* and *native*. Christianity had failed to reform the souls of benighted Kenya natives. Moral surgery by way of the physical was deemed necessary: the philosophy bears the name of John

Cowan, then Kenya's senior superintendent of prisons. It was put to the test in the notorious case of Hola.

Hola was a concentration camp in Garissa, in Eastern Kenya. It housed those LFA ("Mau Mau") captives who were deemed hardcore, the British label for those who were most consistent in their resistance to the entire system of concentration and British colonial rule. They voiced their grievances. Forced to work on some irrigation schemes, they refused and demanded to be treated as political prisoners, not slaves. They demanded better food and better medical care.

Cowan's plan was put into practice on March 3, 1959. About a hundred LFA political prisoners were selected for moral surgery through forced labor. Two senior officers, the prison's superintendent, Michael Sullivan, and his deputy, Walter Coutts, oversaw the operation, actions planned even "at the risk of someone getting hurt or killed."[7] Eleven men were bludgeoned to death and dozens more maimed in what became known as the Hola Massacre.

The horror! The horror! Even Conrad's Kurtz could see the horror he had wrought in the heart of darkness. But for the colonial regime, the real horror of Hola lay in being caught with blood on its hands. The prison officers had failed to be cautious: "If we are going to sin, we must sin quietly."[8] That advice was given in a 1957 letter from Eric Griffith-Jones, the colony's attorney general, to his boss, Governor Evelyn Baring. The fifty-six-year-old Baring—scion of a banking family who a year later would emerge from this heroic ordeal as the First Baron of Howick of Glendale, KG, GCMG, KCVO—concocted the cover-up. His bureaucratic underlings, all the way down to lowest rank and file, took the cue from the top

and repeated the white lie. The victims had drunk contami-
nated water. They were susceptible to scurvy. And the injuries?
British torturers are trained Christian surgeons: they butcher
to heal, not to kill. In fact, the men did not succumb to bruis-
es and broken skulls. At an inquiry later, Walter Coutts, one
of the two overseers of torture, summed it up: the men had
willed themselves to death. Blixen, the gentle baroness from
Denmark, had said it happens to creatures of the wild.

The theory had worked as a cover-up for countless cases
before but not for the Hola Massacre of March 3, 1959. It
became the subject of parliamentary debate in Britain. Even
London acknowledged that British officers had done it. Governor Baring, author of the contaminated-water fable, was
eventually forced to admit that the injuries had come from the
surgical tools of heavy sticks, batons, and boots. But Kenyans
did not need the debate to know. Nearly every family in Central Kenya had a "hardcore" relative or neighbor.

In our own, we had one who carried the label. His name
was Gĩcini Ngũgĩ. He was my uncle; he had looked after me
in the days of my first elementary school, Kamandũra. He was
older than me and dropped out of school into the world of a
settler colony. He and my brother Mwangi, aka Good Wallace,
had been arrested trying to procure bullets for guerrilla fighters of the Land and Freedom Army. Good Wallace escaped
into the mountains.[9] Gĩcini escaped mandatory death because
of his youth, but he was locked up in a concentration camp.
Like the hundreds of others, he would not accept that he was
afflicted with dangerous desires, that he needed therapy. He
was labeled hardcore, but he was not among the eleven men
bludgeoned to death.

In William Shakespeare, soon after Macbeth has murdered King Banquo, Lady Macbeth lures her distraught husband back to bed with the assurance: "A little water clears us of this deed: How easy is it, then!"[10] The Macbeths try to wash away the evidence of their guilt with a little water. The colonial state tried to wash away the evidence of its guilt by changing the name of the place from Hola to Galore. The simple turned complex: the Hola Massacre unmasked the facade of law, order, and civilization the colony had put up for the world to see. Still the state tried to soldier on as if indeed a little water had washed away the blood on the hand.

But Hola did mark a movement of sorts. On April 14, Jomo Kenyatta, the leader of the political wing of the anticolonial resistance, who in 1952 had been convicted of managing Mau Mau and imprisoned for eight years in Laukitang, was now moved to Lodwar. Was this step a harbinger of changes to come? The gesture replaced Hola in the headlines, but it didn't halt the horror or the nightmare that stalked the land.

II

The nightmare was embodied in one figure, a kind of bogeyman of children's stories, only he was real, and he was white, and he was British, and adults feared him. Ubiquitous, able to make simultaneous appearances in different places at the same time, he was a rogue demon, a law unto himself.

Nobody seemed to know his real English name. Everyone knew him as Waitina and spoke of him in the same breath with the white officers commanding administrative police and Home Guards.

The Home Guard was a British creation, a low-paid auxiliary fighting force made up of natives. In January 1953, Major General Sir William Loony Hinde put the auxiliary force under district officers, the lowest white administrative rank deployed in every district. Thus Hinde had given himself an army of vigilantes outside the direct command of the regular army. Was the lawless lawman a district officer and Waitina his generic name or that of the soldiers under him?

Clearly it was not a generic name for every district officer or every British soldier. The British soldier was known as Njoni for Johnny; and the district officer, Ndiũũ, for DO. The solution to the mystery lay in the nickname: Waitina is sometimes translated as "one with big buttocks," but the name literally means "the one related to asshole" or "a relative of anus." Waitina referred to a white boss who took men and women by force. It was the name for a sodomist, most likely a district officer or police officer, because these were there in every district in Kenya.

Rape was a weapon of war; it may have been a sin, but who cared as long as the sinner sinned quietly and the sinned against were too traumatized to proclaim their sexual victimhood openly? But the victims could put out a warning through the generic Waitina.

It was said that Waitina, the ubiquitous lawless lawman, collected body parts of his victims: hands, ears, eyes, male genitals. Or rather his underlings brought them to him in baskets or even in sisal bags. Proof of the kill, it was said, but there were hints that he did more sinister things with the body parts.

The collection of body parts as proof of the kill was not

confined to the white Waitina, whoever he was. Years later it would emerge that one black soldier in the King's African Rifles, but originally from Uganda, distinguished himself not by his height of six feet four inches but by the quantity of body parts he regularly brought to his British superiors. He took no prisoners; their decapitated heads were more valuable than the words their mouths might tell. His zeal against LFA soldiers or suspects earned quick promotions; he rose from private through corporal to sergeant. His name was Idi Amin. The British relocated their man from Kenya back to Uganda in 1959.

Three years before, another Ugandan who had moved to Kenya, in 1950 after expulsion from Makerere College for his anticolonial activities, had also returned to Uganda. His name was Apollo Obote. In Kenya, he had worked his way from laborer for Mowlem Construction Company to a salesman for an oil company, worked with trade unions, and then returned home in 1956 to join the anticolonial Uganda National Congress.

The Congress was formed in 1952 by Ignatius Musazi following the ban of the Uganda Farmers Union in 1949, after it was accused of organizing the riots of the same year over the Asian monopoly of cotton ginning, among other grievances. The simmering effects might have been part of what fueled the 1958 Baganda boycott of Asian shops, two years after the return of the Anti-British Makerere Man and one year before that of the Pro-British Military Man.

The lives of the two men had shadowed each other. Idi Amin Dada was born in Koboko, West Nile, Northern Uganda, in August 1925; Obote, in Akokoro, Lango, Northern Uganda, in December 1925. Lango and West Nile neighbored each other. Both men had worked in Kenya but on the opposite sides of the struggle: Obote with the pro-LFA Kenya African Union; Amin, with the anti-LFA British forces. The two men, with their different experiences of Kenya, had returned to Uganda at about the same time.

In 1959 the British promoted Idi Amin yet again, to warrant officer, the highest military rank for an African in the British Army at the time. The same year, Obote split with the Uganda National Congress and formed the more militant Uganda People's Congress.

The year may have seen this and even more dramatic events that played out publicly on the world stage—the ouster of Batista in Cuba and the rise of Fidel Castro; Hawaii incorporated as the fiftieth state of the United States; Leakey's discovery of *Zinjanthropus*, the 1.75-million-year-old skull of a human ancestor, at Olduvai Gorge in Tanzania; Charles de Gaulle's coming into power in France, dogged by Algerian politics—but for me, it was the year that I, a subject from British colonized Kenya, got on a train bound for Makerere, in neighboring British Protected Uganda. Both were colonies, of course. Only that one, mine, was a wounded land, while Uganda, though exploited, had not been wounded by white settlerdom.

3

Reds and Blacks

I

It is the end of June 1959, and it's like a dream. I board the train at Limuru, the same station that four years back had seen me shed tears of despair when the officials would not let me get on the train bound for Alliance High School because I did not have a permit to travel to another region as then required by the martial laws that regulated African travel within. I had to be smuggled into another train by a sympathetic lower ranking officer. Now, four years later, I am boarding another train bound, not for any region within the country but for the neighboring territory. And as in the past, my mother remains my anchor. Ever since she first sent me to school twelve years back, she has always wanted me to venture, to see what's out there.

I am leaving the colonial Kenya of terror and uncertainty but also the country of my private dreams and desires. Among the many who have come to see me off is Minneh Nyambura, whose smiling eyes make my heart beat so loudly I think people around me can hear the boom. A week or so earlier, we had made a secret soul pact.

II

On the first of July I woke up from the liminal space between private dreams and public nightmares into that of a moving train[1] that hooted ESCAPE, AT LAST, ESCAPE, in my mind at least. My previous train journeys had been between my home in Limuru and my high school in Kikuyu, and I traveled third class. Now I was in second class, going from the known to an unknown, but the unknown felt more welcoming than the known. Besides, I had the company of others with whom I had schooled at the Alliance High.

Some, like me, knew college only as a dream, but others, who had graduated from Alliance to Makerere before us, had already experienced its life and seemed eager to display their college ways to the neophytes. Alcohol was the rite of passage from the rawness of school to the ripeness of college. The transformation was remarkable, in a way. Those whom I had known as pious and exemplary dwellers of Alliance would open beer bottles with the insouciance of seasoned drinkers.

There was a performance element to it, the opening salvo in the pressure to conform. For it soon became apparent that it was not enough for them to display the fact that within a year of college, they had left their high school life behind them; they seemed more eager to use the occasion of a second-class passenger train to initiate the novices into life.

They passed the beer around, some of my fellow neophytes eagerly draining the glasses. I had never tasted brewed beer in my life. The only taste of alcohol I had had was of the home-made mũratina, a kind of wine made from honey and yeast. I declined their offer. Just taste it, one of them asked me. Njĩhia had been a year ahead of me at Alliance but now behaved as if he had seen the light by simply having done a year at college and was on a mission to rescue me from Plato's cave. The more I refused to see the light of the alcohol, the more insistent Njĩhia became, alternating his praises to the beer, which left a moustache of white foam above his upper lip, with mockery of my pretense at innocence and accusations that I was trying to appear holier than they. You are out of school, no longer a baby under headmaster Carey Francis. Still I refused to touch the glass even.

Stung by my continued refusal, Njĩhia suddenly rose from his seat and tried to force the drink on me. It spilled on my clothes. It now became a physical altercation. The others separated us. It was not the most pleasant way of experiencing second-class travel as a prospective college student, but I was glad I had stood my ground. My mother had brought me up to withstand any peer pressure that called on me to do that which otherwise revolted me. This trait would later help me to stand up for what I thought was right despite pressure to succumb to the current and popular. When later in college I drank, it was to satisfy my social needs, not to prove anything to my peers.

Freed from participating in the alcohol-mediated merriment, I sat by the window and looked out. The window framed the view of a continually vanishing presence. It was a series of landscape paintings of infinite varieties of color, size, and shape, from hills, valleys, rocks, thickets, and forests to the sprawling white-settler ranches, wheat fields, and coffee plantations.

And then it struck me. It was this very railway that had opened this rich and varied land to the white settlement. The

stations and towns we passed, from Limuru through Nakuru and Eldoret to those near the border between Kenya and
Uganda, came with the railway line built from 1899 to 1903.
Blood had been spilt by proponents and opponents of the railway. The Koitalel-led Nandi resistance to the construction of
the railway line and the colonial army suppressing the resistance were harbingers of the current LFA-led armed struggle
of which my brother Good Wallace and Uncle Gĩcini Ngũgĩ
were part. The sprawling rolling hills and fields of coffee and
wheat the railway line generated spoke of white presence, but
they also spoke eloquently of African loss. I was benefiting
from a history that had come to negate my history.

At Tororo we crossed from terror-ridden Kenya on one side
to a kind of promised land on the other side of the border
town.

III

Even the land we entered after crossing the border into Uganda seemed enwrapped in a nimbus. The tidy manicured tea
plantations of Limuru and Kericho in Kenya were replaced
by Uganda coffee plants and bananas that seemed to grow in
the freedom of the wild and yet carried full bunches. The vast
verdure before us, all African owned, was breathtaking in its
extravagant display of untrimmed tropical luxuriance.

Such must have been the scenery that greeted writer Winston Churchill when, in 1908, on his first African journey, he
finally left the Kenya of cantankerous British colonial settlerdom and crossed into the British-protected African kingdom:
"Uganda is from end to end a 'beautiful garden' where the

'staple food' of the people grows almost without labour. . . . Does it not sound like a paradise on earth?"[2] And in summary, "Uganda is the pearl (of Africa)."[3]

The only interregnum to my view of the wild verdure was the Indian Madhvani's sugar plantations in Jinja, but even these, seen through the windows of the second-class coaches, came across as green blades dancing in the wind. It was also my first encounter with an Indian-owned and -managed plantation. In Kenya, Indians, by law, were not allowed to own land—this despite their having helped build the railway from Mombasa to Kampala. But in Uganda, it was a different story as evidenced by the Madhvanis. Past the sugar, it was a sudden reentry into the rich tropical lushness, a continuation of Churchill's beautiful garden.

Churchill had erased human presence from the Ugandan landscape. But when fifty years later I reemerged from the garden into the city at the railway station in Kibuli, it was into a human bustle and hustle of black presence selling matokes, potatoes, peanuts, clearly the fruits of their hands on their own soil. Black Baganda women in flowing *busutis* and black men in white *kanzus* and regular Western attire dominated the streets. Even the sight of Indians outside their shops along either side of the city streets added rather than took way from this incredible sight of black people who did not walk as if they were strangers in their city. Kenyan cities and towns always gave off an air of segregation and tension. Here there seemed more ease in the urban racial mingling, among the Asians and Africans particularly. There were no visible effects of the trade boycott of the year before. Absent, even among the few white bodies, was the armed swagger of the Kenya settler.

It was my first encounter with a modern city dominated by black presence, and it was strangely exhilarating. More personal, I had finally entered the capital of a country about which, for as early as I could recall, I had sung, To-Uga-nda, in rhythm with sounds of metal on metal of the trains bound for Kampala and the Baganda Kingdom.

Years later the train and its sounds would still ring in the prose of my fictional world, in the novel *A Grain of Wheat*, in particular. The fact is, the railway, built in the 1890s, the high noon of the imperial Scramble for Africa, had an impact on the economy, politics, culture, and life of the region so profound as to make it inseparable from the history of modern East Africa. A product of British imperial dreams, the train had landed me in the city of my dreams.

The bus from Wadegeya was a slow-motion climb to a biblical city on a hill, except that this city was here and now, and it had a real name, Makerere University College.

IV

Red greeted us on Makerere Hill. Red flowing in the wind. Red-gowned students on all the paths across the campus. I was assigned to Northcote Hall for residency, and even there, I was greeted by men in red. Sir Geoffrey Northcote, after whom the hall was named on its completion in 1952, was former governor of Hong Kong and had been chairman of the University Council at the time of his death in 1948.

Makerere was several times bigger than the Alliance High School campus in Kikuyu, which I had known for the last four years. But it was the red gown, not the buildings, that domi-

Red-gowned students in front of Makerere University's
Main Building

nated the visual landscape. Occasionally black gowns would
flit across, breaking the uniform red, but these were few and
far between. The black gowns signaled professors—lecturers,
as they were called. For me both the red and the black signaled
learning itself.

For a few days, we, the newcomers, in our regular clothes, looked every inch the outsider, ignorami, pretenders to the learning throne, but not a day too soon, we got our share of the red. It felt good. Learning swaddled in red had descended upon us.

No, not so fast, some of the seniors told us. We had not yet joined the celestial company of the anointed. We had yet to take an oath.

Oath? To me, a Kenyan, the word conjured death, destruction, and Hola massacres. I recalled the encounters I had had with the armed enforcers of the Emergency laws of Kenya trying to prove that I had not yet taken the oath of allegiance to LFA. But thousands others had taken the oath for land and freedom, and for that, or even on the suspicion alone, they still languished in concentration camps. Jomo Kenyatta and four of the Kapenguria Five,[4] convicted of managing "Mau Mau" and administering the oath, were still held in Lodwar despite having served their term in prison. The eleven men at Hola had been bludgeoned to death only four months back because they would not acknowledge having taken the oath. And here, at Makerere, in this high seat of learning, they were telling me I would not become a member of the elect unless I took an oath.

Even the Queen of England, judges, the military brass, they all take oaths of office, someone explained. Yes, yes, but none had gone to prison or had his body parts severed on account of it.

The dreaded oathing ceremony turned out to be a grand affair with red-gowned neophytes descending on Main Hall from the four points of the campus. There was an interesting visual division. All the Reds were Africans and Asians; nearly all the Blacks were white Europeans. Whites in black at the front, on the dais; Blacks in red on the floor, facing them.

The academic registrar, Mr. Paul Vowles, administered the pledge: "I promise to seek the truth and study diligently; to obey the principal and all to whom obedience is due; and to keep the principles of the college." Simple words, really, which we repeated after him with all the solemnity of a religious vow. A few prep words and we were done, but the vow continued vibrating in the mind: seek the truth.

What is truth? said jesting Pilate, and would not stay for an answer. This I would read later in Francis Bacon's "Of Truth," in my English class. At Alliance the word *truth* was always in the air. But there, it was a more like a preexisting entity; all we had to do was accept it. In fact, all we had to do to possess it was to kneel before the Cross. No, not possess it but let it possess us, a civilized spirit possession. One Truth for all. Unchanging. Eternal. It was a faith-dependent Truth.

This one to which we had just committed ourselves felt different, a process, closer to what I would later read in Aristotle: "The investigation of the truth is in one way hard, in another easy. An indication of this is found in the fact that no one is able to attain the truth adequately, while, on the other hand, we do not collectively fail, but every one says something true about the nature of things, and while individually we contribute little or nothing to the truth, by the union of all a considerable amount is amassed."[5]

Perhaps if I had read about how Giordano Bruno was burned at the stake at a central Roman square on February 17, 1600, for holding opinions contrary to the Roman Catholic faith, or that twenty-year-old Scottish student Thomas Aiken-head was hanged on January 8, 1697, for holding truths con-trary to those of the Presbyterian Church, I might have react-ed differently.

For now, it was exhilarating, as if after living in a land of one truth, a colonial truth, I had affirmed the right to ask questions and contribute to a common pool of knowledge.

V

There were other rites of passage, social mostly, but nothing would beat my first night at a social evening in Northcote Hall. I would later learn that each hall organized its socials at different times. I assumed it was some kind of after-dinner party with students playing cards, chess, checkers, and table tennis or maybe a concert evening with students performing jokes and stories. I should have asked my seniors, but even then nothing would have prepared me for the night.

It was not simply the transformation of the dining hall into a dance arena that first ignited the excitement, but even more the sight of a real live band on the stage normally occupied by the high table. Apparently every social included live music, more often than not from Peter Nazareth's band. Made up of only those students who could afford to buy their own instruments, it was first named Teddy Bear, after Elvis, before members set-tled on the Makerere Jazz Band. In the tradition of jazz, they had to be innovative and supplemented what they had by mak-ing their bass out of a tea chest with a broomstick and a cord attached, an idea they developed from skiffle musicians. But on this night Northcote had attracted a band from the town.

Northcoters, all men, were the first to arrive, some in three-piece suits but nearly all in ties and bow ties, hanging around in groups, and then, suddenly the excitement. Buses carrying ladies, mostly nurses, from Mulago and Mengo hospitals, had arrived, and the ladies trooped in. The pattern, I would later learn, never changed, year in, year out; only the players changed, graduations replaced by new admissions. The girls would be brought in there in a rented bus, stay for the duration of the dance party, and then be taken back to their lairs in the hospital. Don't be fooled: the ladies were not in the white uniform of nurses, and the scent that filled the air had nothing in common with the smell of hospital.

At Alliance the nearest to this glamorous presence were the Scottish country dances on grass lawns. In the village, it had been the feet of young men in their everyday, in huts badly lit with paraffin lamps, raising dust by themselves, so few women there were who would venture to such places at night. One guitar and one or two human voices provided the music. Men would dance in pairs, but mostly it was solo versus solo in moves that were more acrobatic than the feline motions on a ballroom floor. And now, on the Hill, Makerere Hill, this!

High heeled girls of Mengo and Mulago
In low cuts of half-sleeved and sleeveless dresses
Skirts adorned with shimmering beads
Necks bedecked with glittering jewelry
The looks of sheer delight on suited men
Who hold them close in waltz tango and foxtrot
Oh the grace of solemn pairs gliding on the floor

After every dance, the men would lead their glamorous partners back to the seats arranged against the four walls. Men
remained standing in groups waiting for the next dance. Then
suddenly the groups would break up, individuals gliding
toward the walls to ask for a dance from a different lady.

We the neophytes also sat or stood in groups watching all
this and daring each other to be the first to make a move. The
ladies never seemed to say no, and they all came here to dance,
collective guests, of us, the collective hosts, so why not play
our role? It took some time before one of us gathered the courage to approach the glamorous presence. The success of the
first one to break the self-imposed inhibition emboldened the
others.

I had not taken into account the possibility of my nose
becoming captive to the scent of perfume and my eyes that of
what showed just above the low-cuts. I fought back the desire
to simply stand and stare; and so instead of trying to keep up
with moves I knew nothing about, I was soon stepping on my
partner's feet. When the dance was over, she didn't wait for
me to escort her back to her seat. Later when we neophytes
exchanged reviews, I was struck by the similarities of our
experience. Stepping on the feet of our partners was the common theme. The other was the sheer embarrassment afterward
when we tried to go back for another dance with our previous
victims and they froze us with icy looks or a slight shake of the
head or by suddenly looking down or talking animatedly to
their neighbor at our approach! Clearly we all suffered from
the same malady. The seniors told us of the cure: MABADA.
The Makerere Ball Room Dancing Association.

Of all the clubs and associations on the Hill, MABADA had the largest membership. The best part was the dance lessons the seniors offered new members. The dances, I discovered, were not in the freewheeling style of our village dances. These were very formalized affairs: from the posture, where and how to stand, to counting steps to the left, right, forward. Initially we practiced with pillows, holding them as if they were our partners. Then came the pairing, one man being the pilot and the other the piloted by turns. Eventually we were ready for the first trial of our skills.

It was a MABADA-organized event at the Main Hall. Everything about the event, open to all, was in every way larger and more daunting than anything that we had seen in the halls. This time the ladies came from all the women centers, mostly hospitals, in and around Kampala. Faculty, too. Many people came partnered with wives, husbands, or girlfriends. The seating areas were all outside the dancing hall, in the open. My first night of dance as a MABADA graduate was also a test case of nerve and footwork. Once again it was the waltz, tango, and foxtrot that dominated the floor. It was so exhilarating to dance without stepping on your partner's feet:

> *Then suddenly comes samba or rock and roll*
> *And statuesque pairs break loose*
> *But it's the Lingala music from the Congo*
> *That finally conquers the Ballroom part of*
> *Makerere Ballroom Dancing Association*
> *Bodies become loose and float and fly*
> *As if seeking freedom from gravity*

Even then there were still a few things to learn. If three or more ladies sit at the same table and the first one rejects your hand, then you don't ask the others, for they will certainly say no. You go to a different table farthest from the scene of first rejection and try your luck there. Nothing personal, just the playing out of group dynamics.

Having mastered the ins and outs and formalities of the social evening and the Makerere dance floor, it was time to test what one was made of by going to a nightclub: Top Life near Mengo and later Suzana in Nakulabye. The social evenings had been confined to hall membership. The MABADA dances attracted the elite in and outside the Hill. But the nightclub brought together the mighty and the low, Makerere and the city, the partnered and the unpartnered. The resident or visiting band was bigger, with a whole array of instruments. Neon lights added to the intimacy, mystery, and wonder. This was the real thing:

> Triumphant notes of the trumpet
> Saucy sexy sounds of the saxophone
> Cymbals piano xylophone
> Maraca rattles and drum beats
> Guitar strings from the bass to soprano spring
>   surprise
> Haunting calls of horns and clarinet
> They talk they challenge they moan
> Sometimes they go solo
> Each taking the center the others supporting
> Then all come together and cry and groan and scream

Body captives of sound mass together on the floor
Winged with desire they swing sway sweat and swoon
Oh oh oh step up this step
Oh oh oh this step must never stop
Oh oh oh oh oh oh oh oh

Cigarette smoke and stale smell of beer
Cover bodies crooning in corners

But soon too soon or so it seems the sound fades to
 silence
Reluctant relaxed bodies saunter to the seats
They laugh and shout and whisper and drink
Hearts throb for the next round of sound in sync

Friday or Saturday nights were the best for nightclubbing. One had a whole Sunday to nurse a hangover and, for the religiously inclined, to attend chapels to seek forgiveness for sins committed under the influence.

VI

The faculty seemed supportive of the view of truth seeking that we had sworn to. They encouraged us to develop our viewpoints, not regurgitate theirs or faithfully reproduce what we read in books—the difference between high school and college, they added. In school they spoon-fed you; in college, you held the spoon and fed yourself.

I didn't need the homilies. I took the vow seriously, and

it affected my attitude to books and classes. I would judge myself not by the grade I got but by the bar that I would set for myself. Nothing drastic about this; it was a restatement of my mother's question: Is that the best? But now I had taken a vow to pursue the ideal, to track down truth wherever it might lead me on the road to the best.

I soon discovered, within the first year, that not every faculty member held this rosy view of the quest. In the first year, I took courses in history, English, economics, and the optional religious studies. I had had an on-and-off love affair with the Bible, a book in which Blake's marriage of heaven and hell was consummated in terror and promise. I had also hoped that the course would be a study of religion in general, African and Eastern included.

Christianity, divided into Catholics and Protestants, was the dominant religion on the Hill. There were a very few Muslims, but they had to borrow space for their worship. There were two chaplains and chapels: Reverend Denis Payne for Saint Francis and Father Paul Foster for Saint Augustine. Payne was Anglican but served all Protestants; Foster was a Benedictine but served all the Roman Catholics. Nothing could be more different than their personalities: Payne, shy, sly, and feisty but seemingly humble; Foster, fast, affable, and flamboyant but seemingly understanding.

The religious studies turned out to be a study of Christianity only. Lectures for the academic part were shared between the Benedictine Catholic and the Anglican priests. It was the "humble" Payne whose intellectual intolerance first came out, during his discourse on the Reformation. He mentioned the ninety-five theses that Martin Luther pinned on a church door criticizing the abuses of indulgence and other ills, and of course the Counter-Reformation with the 1545 Council of Trent.

I had been baptized a Protestant of the Scottish variety, but during a discussion that followed Payne's lecture on the Reformation, I said that on evidence it seemed that the Roman Catholic had the correct position. How could a politician, a king or queen in the case of the Anglican Church, become the head of a religious institution? There were times, of course, when popes commanded crowns, armies, and harems. To me, at least, it seemed a clear case of continued mixing of politics and religion—the very practice the architects of the Protestant Reformation seemed to be waxing angry about. I was not taking sides, but we were in college bound by a common oath in a quest for the truth, right? And this was an academic debate, right? Rev. Payne did not see it that way. He stopped the discussion to give a sermon on how one could become a Catholic if one wanted; he had worked out a procedure with his Benedictine counterpart. I had not told the man that I wanted to change denominational allegiance.

His attitude reminded me of a similar reaction from one of my teachers at Alliance, who became hostile when, in response to his claim that Jesus spoke very simple English, I pointed out that Jesus spoke Aramaic. I had not taken kindly to Mr. Smith of the Alliance High School, but I couldn't opt out of his class. In school, all classes were compulsory and the order of knowledge fixed. But did I have to take it at college and for an elective? I never went back to Payne's class. That was my first exercise of my academic and religious freedom, and it felt good.

Three years later, it would be the turn of the flamboyant affable Foster to come out of the pages of Plato and fly his true racial colors. He didn't confine his narrow-minded view of the universe to the classroom. Apparently he never let it intrude into his lectures on Greek thought, or it may have been camouflaged by his social flashiness, but in 1962 he let it all show in a book he titled *White to Move*, published in the United Kingdom to modest critical acclaim. As if he had read Carothers and Cartwright and imbibed their uncanny ability to read black minds, Foster told hilarious stories of his African students who would never answer a straight question with a straight answer. Asked about that bird on that tree, they would talk about a tree on a hill near their home. It was his way of saying that logic and rationality were alien to the African mind. His students, who had worshipped him as this free, liberal, broadminded thinker and writer, with a strong liking for Africa and Africans, were pained and furious when they read how Foster had seen them. They had hugged him as a fellow human; he had embraced them as black objects of his colonial anthropological gaze.

In contrast to both the sly shy but feisty Payne, who shunned difficult questions, and the flamboyant affable Foster, who fooled foe and friend alike, was the Reverend Fred Welbourne, who lived out his name in his friendly and sensitive interactions with students and faculty. Welbourne, warden of Mitchell Hall, who joined Makerere in 1948 to lecture in physics and physick the souls of the Protestants as the first chaplain of Saint Francis, could have been lifted straight out of the pages of Graham Greene. Even his sartorial tastes, the white Baganda *kanzu*s for robes and the sandals for shoes,

tested orthodox colonial views of priesthood. He was open to
all views on any subject, even on religious matters, devoting
his energies to a study of African religions and beliefs, which,
again, offended orthodox priesthood. How could he call devil
worship a religion, much less devote time to study it? But he
was essentially a Christian believer. On being appointed to
Makerere, he was summoned by the Missionary Society in
London to be told that his mandate was to convert the entire
country to Christianity. I did not have a chance to take Welbourne's classes, but I, like everyone else, knew of him. He was
a missionary with a liberal mission.

Intellectual intolerance and narrow-mindedness were not
confined to chapels and chaplains, as I soon found out in my
class in economics. Economics had two divisions: theory and
history. Dr. Cyril Ehrlich, who taught us economic history,
was short with a head that carried a shiny horseshoe bald spot.
He spent the first twenty minutes of every lecture telling us
how intellectually poor we were and warning us against being
bigheaded. "You think you are very intelligent, just because
you have come to Makerere? You think you know everything
just because of setting foot in a college? You know nothing!"
Then he would rattle on about universities abroad, the high
standards, the expectations. The daily putting down of his
students was worse than anything I had ever put up with in
school. I felt trapped in Ehrlich's class. I couldn't drop out of
a mandatory course without incurring the fatal F. At the end
of the second year were the terminal exams called Preliminary,
and an F in any one of the areas could mean the end of my
educational journey. I soldiered on, but his class didn't feel like
the open society that the vows of academic freedom for truth

had led me to expect. It was in his class that a vague idea of publishing a book as an undergraduate began to form. I would have loved to have shown him that we had what it takes to be who we want to be.

I never met the affable Foster, the expert on the black mind, in class, so for me, Payne and Ehrlich remained the exceptions, not the norm. In English and history, at least, I encountered a faculty tolerant of conflicting views, but who nevertheless made it clear that learning was a discipline, not a series of opinions. There were things called facts, evidence, citation, logic, comparison, and of course organization of material into a coherent argument.

At the other end was Emil Rado, from economics, who in my last years would form a semisecret club of thirteen, drawn from faculty and students. It was a club for those with unique talents, supposedly. But the number had to remain thirteen. Why thirteen? I wondered. Thirteen was supposed to be the unlucky number, for the English at least. When recently I told my son, Mukoma, about this and my puzzlement about the number, he said it was probably derived from Jesus and the twelve disciples! Was Rado the Jesus to our twelve disciples? Probably not quite, for, on leaving Makerere, one ceased to be a member automatically, even the founder. The other members would then elect a replacement from among faculty and students. The thirteen remained but their composition changed. Apart from the exclusive secrecy, I never saw anything out of the ordinary in matters discussed or in the depth of the discussion, nothing different from what prevailed in ordinary nonexclusive gatherings. But that was in my last year at college.

The most consistent in encouraging diversity of views was the pipe-smoking Peter Dane. He also stood out for his close reading of texts. On Dickens's *Great Expectations*, he made the characters, especially Magwitch, the convict, come alive for us. Australia was a penal colony where the English undesirables were deported for life: they could never return to Albion's shores without facing arrest, conviction, and prison. Dane's delineation of Magwitch's elaborate attempts to create his own gentleman in the Pip character, and the temptation to come back to enjoy, though surreptitiously, the sight of his creation, was moving, and without his saying so, Dane made us see the novel in terms of class exclusion and empire. He brought Dickens closer home to us. Colony and Crown, prison and palace, they produced each other. *Great Expectations* became a favorite, and a group of us adopted the name Pip.

When, after the terminal second-year Preliminary exams, I was admitted into the three-year honors program in English, I looked forward to having more time with Peter Dane. But he disappeared from Makerere; later, we heard that he had moved to the University of Auckland, New Zealand, which puzzled me immensely. How could anybody leave Makerere, which we took to be the most highly coveted institution in the world, for an island?

Years later I would meet him again, twice. First in 1984 when at his Auckland University I gave the Robb lectures, which became the book, *Decolonising the Mind,* but I don't recall any interactions on that occasion. The second time was in 2005 when he delivered the encomium on the occasion of the honorary doctorate the same university bestowed upon me. In his talk, he recalled the Makerere days, forty years back, which had a special meaning for him, the job being his first as a university professor.

Over lunch I learned a little about the amazing life journey that led him to that first academic job in Makerere. He was born in Berlin in 1921 to a German father and a Jewish mother. He fled Hitler to the United Kingdom in 1939. The eighteen-year-old youth was interned as an enemy alien in Australia in the 1940s at a camp near Wagga Wagga. After the war, he went back to England, where he met his future wife, Gabriele Herrmann, who nursed him with love back to life and belief. They married in 1945, and in 1956, with her support, he graduated in English from the University of London. She remained the love of his life for fifty years, till he lost her to an illness. At the time I met him in Auckland the second time, he had retired, married the second love of his life, a Maori lady, and still lived in their home in the Bay of Islands.

At lunch I couldn't help but go back to our classes on Dickens's *Great Expectations* in Makerere. I recalled the magic of his Magwitch presentation, but I also recalled that he never said a thing about his own sojourn in Australia. The encounter made me realize how little I knew the Makerere Dane; I had always assumed him to be of English stock, an academic whose life had been books and books and more books.

Though the faculty was largely white, it was actually diverse in cultural backgrounds. In the Department of English alone, there were the Irish Alan and Phyllis Warner; the South Africans, D.D. Stuart, Trevor Whittock, and Murray Carlin; the Scottish Margaret MacPherson; and the taciturn Englishman R. Harris. The English David Cook and Geoffrey Walton would come later.

My encounter with Dane made me look back to my early days in Makerere and wonder what hidden and complex histories my professors may have carried behind the masque of black academic gowns, stern faces, and measured words. It was one of the chroniclers of Makerere, Carol Sicherman, who recently told me that Murray Carlin fought in North Africa, very much animated by a wish, as a South African Jew, to fight the Nazis. The pro-Nazi leanings of some Boers must have been a powerful incentive, and yet at the time of my studies of D.H. Lawrence with him, you could not read this drama from his inscrutable face.

> *Sometimes we wear masks*
> *Not with deceptive intent*
> *Not even to shield faces from the sun*
> *But the within from the without*
> *Or save the day from the gaze of yesterday*
> *We wear masks*
> *The better to dance the big masquerade of just living*

VII

The other inscrutable, on the face at least, was Principal Bernard de Bunsen. We hardly ever interacted with him; we caught only glimpses of him at important ceremonies, so he remained a mystery. But I felt that I already knew him: his name reminded me of the Bunsen burner we used in our labs in school; the initials B.B. could stand for both the burner and the brain. Was he related to Robert Bunsen, the nineteenth-century German chemist and designer of the burner named after him? No way of knowing. It was only when I read his autobiography, *Adventures in Education*, that I learned of his birth, not in Germany, but in the environs of Cambridge, though he graduated from Balliol College, Oxford. His first major job was as director of education in Palestine, not in the Ottoman Empire he had heard about from his mother, but in the British Mandate, "the scene of endless conflict between Arabs and Jews inflamed by the new waves of postwar Jewish immigration from the ghettos and concentration camps of Central and Eastern Europe seeing not only the Homeland that Balfour had promised, but also a Jewish state."[6]

Three months after the end of the British Mandate on May 15, 1948, he was on his way from Jerusalem to Kampala, first as reader and head of the Education Department, then later the principal during my years at Makerere.

The opposite end was one we all thought we knew. Hugh Dinwiddy joined the department and the college in 1956 as lecturer in English. But he made only a few appearances in class; he had more than a handful as the warden of Northcote Hall.

Northcote[7] was one of the six halls of residence, the others being Mitchell, New Hall, Livingstone, and University, all for men, and Mary Stuart for women. Outside the classrooms, departments, and faculties into which the academic learning was organized, the halls were the center of student life. They had their own traditions, cultures, and values, forged in rivalries in social activities, theater, and academic achievements. Identities were in terms of halls of residence.

The rivalries would at times express themselves in the vocabulary of the colonizer and colonized. When New Hall was built, it shared the same warden and administration as the older Northcote. In the parlance of the time, New Hall was spoken of as a colony of the latter. The tension between them was seen as a case of New Hall continually seeking and asserting her independence from Northcote's colonial shadow.

Another "colonial story" involved Mitchell and University halls. Mitchell was one of the oldest residences for men, one of the hostels of its original incarnation as a technical high school. It was named after Sir Philip E. Mitchell, governor of Uganda[8] between 1934 and 1940, who supported the school's early development, envisioning it as a future center of higher education for the East African group of territories, "a place where there shall be provision alike for the sons of the greatest in the land and the poorest,"[9] a vision realized in the Makerere I was now attending. The old Mitchell symbolized the continuity from school to college.

Without a lockable common entrance to the scattered buildings, the newly imported Oxbridge tradition of midnight closures of outside doors by porters or custodians and the exclusion of visitors after the witching hour could not be carried out effectively. The night guard, armed with a stick only, could not apprehend all the curfew offenders. So Mitchellites moved freely at all times of night and day.

Michellite freedom was a comment on the unfreedom in the other halls after midnight. We heard scary stories of students who, coming after the curfew hour, would try to scale the high walls of the modern halls, resulting in death in the case of Northcote. Modernity had its price, it seemed, and Mitchellites were reluctant to embrace it.

When in 1962 it came to shutting the old to build a new, modern Mitchell, it was decided to spread out the residents to the other halls. Mitchellites resented the loss of freedom but more the joke that they would have to undergo orientation because they had never really been civilized. On the night of March 29, 1962, wearing their old gowns, they ate their dinner early; then they ran to University Hall, planted the Mitchell flag on the central table, captured the chairman with a pop-gun, and forced him to sign the charter of surrender they had already had drawn up in gothic script by Glennie Dias, who would end up a Northcoter.

The conditions and terms of surrender stipulated that Mitchell Hall, "hereafter referred to as the colonialists," had conquered and consequently colonized University Hall, "hereinafter known as the natives."

Aware that the natives had acquired only the outward form of culture, the colonial government pledged to impart the essence of civilization to the natives. For this purpose, the colonial power had decided to send 40 (forty) expatriates to live among the natives on condition (a) that the conquered country offer adequate inducement to the expatriates and (b) that on retirement the expatriates shall be entitled to full compensation by the natives for the loss of their career. As part of the overall colonization policy, Mitchell Hall had sent officers to New Hall, Northcote, and Livingstone as part of the AID program to backward countries.

The Makererean, the student newspaper, headlined the facetious incident as University Hall being "invaded, conquered and colonized by the ever expanding Mitchell Hall Empire."

Whatever the sensibilities of the High Table—apparently its members were not amused at the dig at colonialism—the Mitchellites were determined to assert their Mitchellness by going to University Hall as conquerors, not supplicants.[10] They had character to protect and reputation to keep.

Mitchell's case exemplifies the obvious, that each hall had evolved traditions specific to itself and a communal spirit unique to itself. It was not just the students alone: the character of the warden also contributed to shaping the overall direction of the residence. Welbourne's freewheeling character and that of the hall he led reflected each other, some even claiming he was in on the planning stages of the invasion.

Dinwiddy, who had taken over the Northcote wardenship from John Coleman in 1956, was a Roman Catholic who, unlike Father Foster, embodied a truly catholic culture. His character was forged in the academy and in sports. A graduate of Cambridge, he was a first-class cricketer, having played for the Kent County Cricket Club (KCCC), played for Cambridge University CC in the 1930s, won blues for Rugby, played for the Harlequins, and even trialed for England in 1936. He loved literature, music, and people and was always fascinated and drawn to individual stories. His hearty laughter was infectious.

Northcote under Dinwiddy attracted all sorts of characters, the enigmatic, the tragic, and the eccentric. The enigmatic, call him Dr. Scout, was a brilliant student of medicine, moreover an Alliance product, a scout leader, Queen's scout even, who used his room in Northcote Hall as headquarters for a vast vehicle theft and robbery operation spanning the Congo, Uganda, Kenya, and Tanganyika. When years later Dr. Scout's thieving ways caught up with him and ruined his flourishing medical practice, those of us who knew him at the time wondered how he could have been able to pass his medical exams while masterminding robberies across international borders.

J. Njoroge was the case of tragic genius. He was probably the most widely and deeply read student of my time on the Hill. He joined Makerere a year after me, and within months of his arrival, he was challenging third-year honors history students on facts and interpretation of European thought and history. He talked of Kant and Hegel and Aquinas and Marx to puzzled students years his senior. Taking the search for truth literally, he talked of doing research and wanted to visit missionary archives in Kampala. He approached the Institute of Social Research at Makerere for help but was dismissed as an upstart: concentrate on your classes and class requirements. He refused to confine himself to English history and argued that it was important to see it in the context of European history. He went to the senior professors, who told him to concentrate on passing his exams in English history. J. Njoroge never studied for exams: for him exams were a test of what he already knew, not of what he had crammed a few weeks before. He always got through with Distinction. He published one paper, "Christianity and the Rise of Nationalism in East Africa" in the journal *The Undergraduate* of March 1962. By then he had become frustrated by what he took to be the intellectual narrow-mindedness of Makerere. He wanted to get out. Privately, he applied and got a scholarship to what he thought was a college of higher education in Paris but on arrival in Paris found it was a kind of vocational college for the French language and flew back. Then he left for Dar es Salaam, enrolled in the newly established law school without officially withdrawing from Makerere, but he became even more frustrated. He returned to Makerere, was expelled for having broken the university regulations, but Dinwiddy fought for him and managed to have the ban reduced to just a three-month suspension. His was the restless mind of a genius, and Dinwiddy seemed to understand. But Njoroge never came back. He fell to a car accident.

I really missed him. He and I used to engage in heated debates over just about everything, from politics to literature, history, journalism, and philosophy. Although I was not his match in European history and philosophy, I more than made it up with my vast knowledge of literature.

The eccentric was Babulal Patel, a brilliant painter who had no formal training or coaching in art. Half deaf and not much interested in the usual academic curricula required to get into college, he found help in Mr. Manohar Lal Sood, principal of Kisumu High School in Kenya, who, recognizing Babulal's unique talent, appealed and got him admitted to Makerere Fine Arts Department. Patel readily found a home in Northcote, but he chose to work under the shade of a tree, stripped to his underwear. He would paint multilimbed figures inspired by the Indian epics, with bold green or blue colors that one could not erase from memory. Sometimes he would disappear without telling anybody, but Dinwiddy would somehow find him, mainly in the bushes around, and would lure him back to the hall. He was the perfect example of the Platonic "mad" genius.

That was Dinwiddy! He brought the friendly but competitive spirit of sports into Northcote culture: he was chief coach, motivator, cheerleader, counselor, and consoler in chief. He was there to see his fighters off, and he would be there to receive them whether they had lost or won. His generous personality helped forge a special Northcotian community spirit to which we became loyal.

He and his pianist partner, Yvonne Marie née Catterall, were literally the head of a Northcote family nurtured by private and public rituals, with Dinwiddy as the chief ritualist. He would personally call on those in difficulty and listen to their problems. He also published the *Northcote Newsletter*, through which he reported and highlighted all aspects of life in the hall and touted our achievements in sports and academic fields. It was written with wit and littered with literary and sports allusions.

Sometimes he would invite the conquering heroes to his house, directly opposite the main entrance of the hall, for a homemade meal, but more often than not, he would invite the student achievers to dine and wine at the High Table.

Northcote's dining hall was multipurpose: a daily eating space, a dance arena for socials, and an art gallery, walls covered with art by hall artists, the most famous being the murals by Sam Ntiro and Ignatius Sserulyo's rendering of the wars of religion in Buganda.

The resident faculty dined at the High Table always, while we students ate from lower tables. But once a week, the high table was a formal affair; the diners dressed in suits and academic gowns. The guests included important players in the Uganda Protectorate administration or any dignitaries visiting from outside Uganda. Among these in my time were Abiola Irele, a budding Paris-based Nigerian intellectual who years later would bloom into one of the leading lights of literary and critical theory; the Kenya governor, Sir Patrick Renison, who infamously described Kenyatta as the leader of darkness and death; and the ex-governor of Uganda, Sir Andrew Cohen, who once exiled the young *kabaka* (king) of Buganda to London before being forced to bring him back. Dinwiddy was at the head of the table, the adorable Yvonne always at his side.

To live in Dinwiddy's Northcote was to be part of something that seemed slightly bigger than oneself. Victory and loss, triumph and disaster engendered a common sense of grief or joy; and even we, the 1959 newcomers to the family, were soon absorbed into the Northcote spirit. If a Northcoter was competing in any arena, we flocked there to cheer him. But nothing—not even sports—compared with the interhall English competition in audience presence and anticipation. One did not have to be a specialist to enjoy a theater performance.

The Interhall English Department Competition for original short plays, short stories, speeches, and poems was initiated by Professor Alan Warner in 1958. His wife, Phyllis, was well known in Makerere and Kampala theater circles and was a key actress in the Makerere Players, an amateur company mainly for expatriate staff on the Hill. Because of the place of English in the academic, intellectual, and cultural life of colonies, this annual interhall competition was the crown jewel of all competitions.

I was among the Northcoters present in the 1960 competition and experienced the humiliating loss of our hall's entry, which came in at the bottom. Jonathan Kariara's *The Green Bean Patch*, with Ben Mkapa, won the coveted first position for New Hall. Years later Kariara managed the Oxford University Press office in Nairobi, and Ben Mkapa became the third president of Tanzania, but then they were happy victors from New Hall, our neighbor. The collective gloom in our hall was palpable in our every gesture.

Something happened inside me. I had never written a play before or even thought of writing one, despite my theater experience at Alliance. But even without saying it to anybody, I knew that I was going to write a one-act play for the next time. My first foot in theater was in response to a community need and hope. Thus was born my first one-act play, *The Rebels*.

The play deals with a male Makerere student from Kenya who falls in love with a local Ugandan girl and gets engaged to her. Their marriage plans are thwarted by the objections of his community, which cannot accept a marriage into a culture that does not circumcise women. He oscillates between the demands of love and the commands of tradition, unable to bring himself to break with the girl or to rebel against his community. The girl makes up his mind for him; she rejects him and contemptuously throws the engagement ring at his feet.

The ending was supposed to be somber, sad with tragic overtones. But Wahome,[II] the boy who acted the girl's part—and made a beautiful girl, at that—decided, against everything we had rehearsed, to wiggle his hips in an exaggerated gesture of contempt, and the entire audience burst into laughter. Up until then, we were doing very well, but that gesture did us in. We took second position, but that was still a great leap from the one we had occupied in recent years.

That was in 1961. I had become a playwright despite myself. Though I had taken part in Shakespearian drama in high school, I had never seen myself as a possible playwright, my literary ambitions being vaguely in the area of fiction. But now circumstances had plunged me into theater first, and my effort at a one-act play, which came in second to Nazareth's *Cosmos*, had earned me the title of playwright. Every Northcoter said I was one. Dinwiddy said so and mentioned my name prominently in his *Northcote Hall Newsletter.* I became my hall's best hope for 1962. I did not disappoint.

I fulfilled the expectations with my second one-act drama, *The Wound in the Heart.*[12] And every Northcoter was happy with our winning the trophy for the entire 1962 Interhall English Competition.

VIII

However, nobody took umbrage at the denial of a national stage for *The Wound in the Heart*—not Dinwiddy, not my mates in Northcote, and not the faculty or students in the English Department. For them the competition was a thing of yesterday, months ago, really.

Nevertheless, the denial intruded into my mind at odd times and places. I was now in my third year, having passed Preliminary exams, the end-of-second-year ordeal, the halfway mark to a degree. Those who failed were discontinued. Those who passed could choose their concentration. I had been accepted into an honors English program, a year longer than for a general degree.

I dropped economics. Bye-bye, Doctor Cyril Ehrlich—no more lectures about students' big heads—but the vague idea of doing something that had not been done, just to show him that I could, remained. I missed history, the other subject, but it didn't matter. Literature, I had come to realize, carried a lot of history, philosophy, and culture of the different periods into which the study of English literature was divided. Some of the secondary reading lists that accompanied particular texts helped me situate literature in the great movement of ideas and social changes of the time.

Not that those connections were often drawn clearly in class. To discuss them further and tease out their implications, Gulzar Nensi, Selina Coelho, Emmanuel Kiwanuka, Bethuel Kurutu, Bahadur Tejani, and I formed our own study group, which met after the official hours. One of us would make a presentation on a self-chosen theme based on a common text; the others would respond. Among our group, a text that had been devoid of life in lectures and classroom seminars generated passion in defense or challenge. I once talked on the topic "King Lear: The God," tracing the movement from his self-conception as divinity to his discovery of his humanity in the storm. Forty years later in an e-mail[13] to me from her home in Oxford, Gulzar Kanji née Nensi could still recall what she called the *King Lear* seminar.

Why then, with all the excitement of learning, did denial of a national stage for a one-act drama bother me so? The play and the competition wouldn't even count toward my degree.

Perhaps if I had remained ignorant of the reason behind it, I might have accepted the refusal. But the phrase, "a British officer cannot do that," riled me. The ban told a lie. Unanswered, the compliance would merely cover up the lie.

The Makerere oath spoke to me, clearly, unequivocally: seek the truth. That was my avowed mission. That was why I was in college. I couldn't reverse the decision of the powers that be, but I could fight back, at the very least contest the monopoly

of the Kampala National Theater by the European community. The big question was how?

The year 1960 had already set in motion a series of events
in the world and Africa that would affect the campus in ways
that would shape my eventual decision and response to the
question.

4

Benzes, Sneakers, Frisbees, and Flags

I

John F. Kennedy, the thirty-fifth president of the United States, was sworn in on January 20, 1961. His challenge, "Ask not what your country can do for you—ask what you can do for your country,"[1] was on the lips of many students on the campus. Not that we had any country on which to make demands or pledge devotion. We were all colonial subjects at the time, and yet somehow the words seemed to speak to us and offer hope that we would soon have countries to which we could make a similar pledge. Kennedy was already a name among us because of the dramatic student airlifts begun after he and our own Tom Mboya met in 1959 at a conference on international affairs.

At twenty-nine, Tom Mboya[2] had risen from a leading trade unionist to a leading figure among the politicians who had emerged in Kenya following Jomo Kenyattta's imprison-ment in 1952. He was among the most fervently admired of the young anticolonial nationalists. Education was the third of their triad of demands, the others being land and freedom. But it was clear, to them that the colonial institutions could not produce enough skilled and educated manpower to meet the challenges of the new Africa heralded by Ghana's independence in 1957. The Mboya-Kennedy airlifts of African students to American universities was meant to close the educational deficit.

Among the first batch of the eighty-one students that landed in New York City on September 11, 1959, were a few from Alliance High School—bright minds, but they had not managed to secure any of the limited spots in Makerere. Thanks to the airlift, Philip Ochieng, my Ping-Pong-playing pal of the past, and I had gone to college the same year, he in the United States and I in Uganda. Among other beneficiaries was Barack Obama Sr., the man who would father the future president, Barack Obama Jr.

The feel-good moment of the educational mass rescue was a healing counterweight to the Hola massacre earlier in the year. Along with themes of eradicating poverty in some of his speeches, the airlifts, which continued throughout the year 1960 and beyond, made Kennedy a voice of the new against old colonial Europe. Young Kenyans readily identified with Kennedy's electoral fortunes and the triumph and ambition of his 1961 inaugural.

The Kennedy moment and momentum inspired other initiatives, including some to Eastern Europe organized by Jaramogi Oginga Odinga. Cold War rivalries affected everything, including offers of school. In addition to a student airlift, what about teacher airlifts to the students?

The idea of Teachers for East Africa, forerunner of the Peace Corps, formally came out of the 1960 Princeton conference sponsored by the African Liaison Committee of the American Council on Education. Years later, the originators of the idea, R. Freeman "Jay" Butts and Karl Bigelow, would be seen in a photo in which Idi Amin, the scourge of local teachers and intellectuals, is smiling at them, but his grin doesn't diminish the animating idealism of the original aim, "to assist East Africa in expanding and developing secondary education and the training of teachers in such a way that East Africa can most rapidly move to supply its own teachers." Nor does it take away from the commitment, dedication, enthusiasm, and friendliness of the individual teachers. They viewed themselves as respondents to the challenges of a new frontier, a sense deepened by the telegram John Kennedy sent to their initial training base at Columbia University, reminding them they were unofficial ambassadors of the United States, for "while in East Africa you will be viewed as representatives of the United States, your values will be considered as its values; your words as its words."[3]

Makerere College was to be the final leg of their training. That was why in 1961 we woke up one day to skies over the green lawns of the Hill filled with "unidentified flying objects" and the ground full of sneakers-wearing aliens trying to catch them.

II

In his book *Adventures in Education*,[4] Bernard de Bunsen, the principal in my time, describes Makerere as a Charing Cross, with a constant flow of visitors, from governors and secretaries of state to world leaders like Indira Gandhi of India and Golda Meir of Israel. Governor Sir Andrew Cohen frequented the dances held at Main Hall.

Makerere attracted not only the scholar, politician, and musician. There was the adventurer also. I remember the German couple, Friedrich and Susan Vogel: they had driven their Mercedes-Benz across North Africa to East Africa, the first leg of their first African journey, which would later take them back to Germany through Central and West Africa. They became guests of Northcote, courtesy of Dinwiddy. Theirs was probably the first Mercedes-Benz on Ugandan soil, in all of East Africa probably. It didn't attract too much wonder or admiration, East Africa then being a British Ford territory, but I did note that the Vogels made their car fairly ubiquitous and conspicuous at public events and took many group photos of themselves and the students around it.

The couple were very pleasant, the opposite of the images of the Germans drawn by the English in their narrative of German colonialism in Tanganyika and South West Africa, and of course World War II. The couple and the warmth they exuded were a far cry from the Germans of the Herero massacres and the Auschwitz gas chambers. They hardly ever talked politics, but spoke more about German philosophy, art, and industry. Still, I always thought of the couple whenever the politics of the Berlin Wall, begun on August 13, 1961, came up in newspapers.

When, fifty years later, they received me in their Munich home overlooking the snowy Alps, I learned that theirs had been a journey prompted less by the waters of the Nile, Congo, Zambezi, or Niger than by the flow of blood in their veins.

Susan had agreed to marry Friedrich on condition that their honeymoon be a drive across Africa, a continent neither had ever visited. He accepted the challenge. They collected all the money they had saved, not much for the newly graduated, and then negotiated a free secondhand Mercedes-Benz from the company. Their romantic journey became also a mobile commercial for the three-point star logo, the global symbol of the Mercedes-Benz brand since the merger of Daimler and Benz in 1926. The name Mercedes was adopted in 1902 at the insistence of the manufacturers' wealthy client, racing driver Emil Jellinek, who wanted his cars to carry the Spanish name of his daughter, Mercedes.

Mercedes Benz soon became the status symbol of the newly emergent elite spawned by Makerere and independence. I wrote short stories, "The Mercedes Funeral" and "Mercedes Tribesmen," satirizing this obsession. Wamabenzi, or the Merceded, became the name of the new postcolonial upper-middle class.

From its inception as a university, Makerere attracted visitors who left their marks here and there in the social life at the campus. However, there was nothing quite like the sneakers-wearing aliens.

III

Call it an American invasion! No sooner did they arrive than they spread across the campus playing catch with monsterlike gloves that swallowed the ball, flinging Frisbees that flew in the air like plates out of space, throwing oval balls to each other and shouting "Hi" to locals. Some wore multicolored baggy shorts and vests and, for footwear, sandals and sneakers, what we called tennis or rubber shoes. This first batch of the aliens was wholly white.

The sartorial difference between them and us was striking. On my first arrival at Makerere in my not-so-smart-looking trousers, my friends had rushed me off to Sayani's Draperies on Kampala Street for a customized gabardine and wool jacket and trousers. Sayani was an Indian tailor who somehow had become the clothes designer for Makerere. Every student was always dressed as if ready for a cocktail party at a moment's notice. The tie completed the wear. I liked a narrow black bowtie with a touch of white at the edges. On solemn occasions, the Americans would turn their casual into formal wear by adding a bow tie in bold colors. The American and the British sartorial traditions were clearly in conflict.

There had been American visitors to Makerere before. In 1959, it was flutist Herbie Mann, courtesy of the State Department; in 1960, Louis Armstrong hosted by Peter Nazareth's Makerere Jazz Club. Both had performed in the Main Hall. But the arrival of the first wave of Teachers for East Africa in June 1961 was altogether different in ways big and small. The teachers were in Makerere for an orientation program and a diploma from the Department of Education, then headed by Professor Eric Lucas. Afterward, they would be sent to African secondary schools in Kenya, Uganda, and Tanzania.

Their adaptability helped them quickly assume the character of the hall of their new residence, while their inventive vigor affected the character of their adopted residence. On the campus as a whole, they changed some old ways of doing things. The first to go was the red gown, slowly at first, but in time the authorities were forced to loosen the requirement of its regular use. Sneakers and sandals began to challenge leather shoes shined to a mirrorlike finish. *The Makererean*, the printed newspaper they introduced, soon replaced the old student news magazine, called the *Guild Information Bulletin*, cyclostyled typed sheets clipped together. Dating, too. American girls with African and Asian boys; American boys with African and Asian girls, or simply American and American. Whatever the pairings, the Americans were more prone to public displays of affection than the local counterparts.

They also ventured into theater, most notably a production of *Macbeth* in African robes. I had seen many Shakespearian productions, at Alliance mostly, but the African actors wore imitations of seventeenth-century English garb. This was a complete novelty. It may have been my previous year's second placement in drama that made Nat Frothingham seek me out, but I agreed to be assistant director. I would take notes on movements and positions; I would contact the actors, and if Nat were absent or engaged elsewhere, I would go over the movements already blocked. I became the production's memory.

Frothingham subsequently became the editor and publisher of the *Montpelier Bridge*, a free community newspaper, and an advocate of Vermont independence, but at Makerere he seemed driven by love of theater more than politics or ideology. Still, he was conscious that the production was a challenge to the status quo. At the Hill, all the previous Shakespeare productions had been by the white faculty grouped around an amateur company, the Makerere Players.

Frothingham was incredibly optimistic and had an infectious energy and enthusiasm that turned the initial skepticism

Scene from *Macbeth*

among some of the actors into belief and commitment. *Macbeth* in African clothes and accents was a success in terms of attendance and the buzz it created. There had not been a

Uganda Argus, "A Courageous Macbeth by Makerere Society,"
November 1961

wholly student production of Shakespeare, much less one in African robes.

He asked me to join him in another production. I declined. I was then in the middle of writing the play *The Wound in the Heart*, whose fortunes would immerse me in the politics of art in a rapidly changing colonial situation whose force and speed had been captured in a memorable image by a British politician a year earlier.

IV

The marquee politician was the Conservative Harold MacMillan whose image of a wind blowing through the continent of Africa became the trope for an unstoppable resurgence of national consciousness.

Context of time and place are as much a part of meaning as the words that carry it. When the "wind of change" speech was first given on January 10, 1960, in Accra, capital of the newly independent Ghana under Kwame Nkrumah, it was applauded, but on February 10 in Pretoria, capital of apartheid South Africa under Hendrick Verwoerd, it was received with stony silence. Soon the silence sounded louder than the applause; the white rejection of the implications of the phrase was as fast and furious as the wind itself.

The South African whites turned the country into a kraal around which they circled wagons of indifference to the cries of shame without and the crisis of resistance within. Sharpening its claws, the apartheid regime perpetrated the Sharpeville Massacre and followed the bloodbath with bans on the African National Congress (ANC) and the Pan-Africanist Congress (PAC), among others, then hurled their leaders, Albert Luthuli and Robert Sobukwe from the contested civic space into the silence of prisons. The jailing of black leaders climaxed with the incarceration of Nelson Mandela in 1962. Four years later, a white Kenyan settler leader, Michael Blundell, titled his autobiography *So Rough a Wind*, clearly echoing the 1960 MacMillan metaphor.

The colonialists had tried to blunt the force of the rough wind by releasing, with dramatic fanfare, the Corfield Report, titled *The Origins and Growth of Mau Mau: An Historical Survey.*[5]

Frank Derek Corfield, whom the State had handpicked in 1957 to write the survey, had as his qualifications governorships in Sudan and Palestine and retirement in Kenya in 1954, where he became secretary of the War Council against "Mau Mau." The partisan "historian" received a handsome sum to come up with footnoted musings about a situation in which he was fully implicated. He did not disappoint: he wrote what was supposedly a factual historical examination of the LFA, entirely from a settler's point of view.

When I left Kenya in 1959, I thought I had escaped the political nightmare that engulfed the land, but the Corfield report, a literary nightmare in its own right, followed me into Uganda. While it created a general stir on the Hill, in me it stirred very personal emotions. I read it through the eyes of my brother Good Wallace and my uncle Gĩcini. I knew they were good men. Both had played a positive role in my schooling. Largely because of them, I could now read the written word, not as a gift horse, but one whose teeth called for critical examination.[6]

But it was my teeth that I clenched and grated when I read in the Corfield report the description of the soldiers of the Land and Freedom Army (Mau Mau) as social misfits; that "the seeds of potential unrest are sown whenever any primitive society is brought into close contact with a more highly civilized society."[7] The community I came from was being described as primitive and atavistic simply because we desired freedom and took measures to make the dream come true. To explain the LFA resistance, Corfield simply and unabashedly harvested from J. C. Carothers's government-commissioned book, *The Psychology of Mau Mau*,[8] which Corfield describes in a footnote as a penetrating document and which he acknowledges having consulted "freely to supplement my own knowledge of the African."[9]

The claim to knowledge of the native mind is a thread that runs through much of European writing on Africa, liberal to conservative. The sources of this expertise were just the fact of contact with natives or animals or both—hence the resort to zoological and forest metaphors. The fact that LFA soldiers were based in the forest makes Corfield observe that "the natural tendency of the wounded animal is to return to its lair."[10]

For his flight-to-forest theory, Corfield also relied on the work of another "authority," the policeman Ian Henderson, who, in his *Hunt for Kimathi*,[11] released in 1958, also claimed to know the African mind and its forest orientation: "If the Kikuyu are the Germans of tribal Kenya, [Dedan] Kimathi was their Hitler," wrote Henderson. "Like Hitler he had to wait until the fabric of society broke around his head, but then he was able to exploit the convulsions with throbbing, burning oratory. Financial chaos and the threat of Communism gave Hitler his chance. The corruption of Kikuyu customs by Mau Mau and the flight to the forest gave Kimathi his opportunity."[12]

In his account of the LFA, Henderson had relied on Carothers's psychology. And now Corfield had used Henderson to corroborate what he got from Carothers. Carothers, Corfield, and Henderson become co-authors of the same pseudoscience, the twentieth-century heirs of Samuel Cartwright, the nineteenth-century physician of the slave plantation. Clearly, here was a case of the colony projecting its practices onto the resisting other. The LFA did not invent massacres, strategic villages, concentration camps, public mass hangings, and the torture chambers that proliferated in the cities and villages.

How did a colonial student ever survive the daily bombardment of this condescending view of my history and being? The journey of a colonial student is marked with failed attempts, but also victories. Even then, scars may remain. They are to be found in some of my outlook and tone at the time. One can only hope the scars don't hide festering wounds. Luckily for me, I loved books. Books can enlighten but can also benight, but at least one can play one off against another. Makerere taught me to value books even more; her well-endowed library became my second residence. In the library, I was the lord of the intellectual manor with a hierarchy of willing and dedicated staff ready to serve me.

That was how I stumbled upon Norman Leys's *Kenya*. This Glasgow University–trained doctor questioned the colonialism he served. Not the least of my fascination was the fact that he wrote of what he observed between 1902 and 1920, without once claiming to know the African mind. He was the answer to Corfield, years before that emissary of colonialism came to the scene.

Leys's book had several gems for me, and I duly wrote them down as if the fact of trapping them with my handwriting would make them yield the answers I sought. For example:

That a European should land in Africa with 50,000 pounds and multiply that sum tenfold, partly no doubt by his own exertions but mainly by the sale for 200,000 pounds of land he had got from the government for nothing, and by using the kind of offices in inducing the natives of the country to work for him, this seems to the government one admirable proceeding.[13]

This was the exact opposite of the dominant official narrative of Kenya's history as the actions of a band of white idealists on sparsely populated wilderness, a view given a veneer of scholarship in Elspeth Huxley's *White Highlands: Delamere and the Making of Modern Kenya*.[14] Corfield consulted Elspeth Huxley and ignored Norman Leys.

My mother, whose impact on my intellectual life can never be told enough, used to be very hard on us when we children told adults to their face that they lied. This was the one admonition I never understood. Grown-ups lied all the time. But still recalling her concerns, I would ask myself: How does a grown man, an adult, a governor even, literally sit down and consciously fabricate lies and sleep in bed untroubled by his inventions? Corfield had even trashed the efforts the Kenyan people had put into building their own schools, an effort to which I was a living witness.

I was a proud product of the Kikuyu Independent Schools Movement, whose ban and destruction by the colonial state Corfield saw fit to celebrate. If he had honestly consulted Leys's *Kenya*, he could have come across another gem about the vast discrepancies in the resources allocated to a white European child and an African child: "The government educational policy is revealed most clearly by the fact that it proposes to spend on new school buildings alone for the 1500 European children in the colony more than its total expenditure on the education of African children during the last five years."[15] Indeed as early as 1924, this doctor had predicted an armed revolt, in another gem: "The whole European colony is organized for defense against African rebellion, while, except for troops and police with European officers, Africans and Indians are unarmed. . . . But will Africans in Kenya always submit passively to the system of life we have imposed on them?"[16]

The Land and Freedom Army answered the question in 1952 with its actions. The colonial state tried to obscure the clarity in the name with the meaningless mumbo-jumbo "Mau Mau." The alliterative Mau Mau was based on a deliberate, or inadvertent, rendering of the equally alliterative *muma*, as in *muma wa (gwĩtia) ithaka na wĩyathi*, "Oath of unity for (demanding) Land and Freedom. The proper name of the political arm of the movement was Kĩama kĩa Muma, the Muma Movement, and of its fighting wing, Mbũtũ ya Kũrũĩra Ithaka na Wĩyathi, the Land and Freedom Army. Their motto was *Maũndũ no merĩ: ithaka na wĩyathi*, Two absolute demands: land and freedom.

In Makerere, Reverend Fred Welbourne gathered a group of Kenyan students for weekly discussions on the Corfield Report. I was not in the circle, but I eagerly awaited the results, eventually published under the title, *Comment on Corfield*.[17] The group's well-considered responses and observations were marred only by their talking of "Mau Mau" as if it was also a form of religion. But the LFA was not a religious movement, any more than the Conservative or Labour parties in Britain were Christian for saying prayers and swearing on the bible.

Whatever their shortcomings, the year-long discussions showed once again that, by the very fact of its position on a hill literally and metaphorically, the college could not avoid the effects of the political winds blowing across the continent. Makerere was like a vane registering the direction and intensity of the wind.

V

In its own way, the Makerere Students Guild, founded in 1954 with the Malawian J. David Rubadiri as the first president, had all along anticipated the changing colonial situation. At a time when the entire imperial world denied Africans the vote, the officers of the students' governing body were elected in a secret ballot on the basis of one student, one vote. Elections involved campaigns for votes, climaxing in debates among the contending candidates in front of the entire assembly. The victorious president drew his cabinet from the Students' Representative Council, later called the Makerere Students' Guild, made up of delegates from the different halls of residence elected the same way. The guild was a democracy in an otherwise absolutist colonial system. It was pan-African in composition, reflecting the multinational character of the student body. Between 1954, when it was born, and 1963, the Makerere Students Guild had presidents from Malawi, Kenya, Tanzania, and Uganda.[18]

I was the delegate from Northcote and became the guild information officer in the Ombati government, 1961–62, but resigned later over disagreement about financing *The Makererean*. I supported the principle of *The Makererean* being financed by the guild but retaining editorial independence, whereas others thought it should be under the broad control of the guild, an updated form of the *Guild Information Bulletin*. They did not want to finance a rogue institution.

The guild marked the different phases of a rapidly changing situation. Barely three years after it was formed, the guild was celebrating Ghana's independence in 1957. In 1958, it organized the first Pan-African Students' Conference, with delegates from eleven countries, at which Tom Mboya was the main speaker.[19]

Nigerian independence followed in 1960. But the independence that most defined the early sixties was that of the Congo. The wind of change blowing in the Congo became a hurricane that left in disarray everything in its path.

VI

Patrice Lumumba's and Kennedy's rise to power were similar. The two men campaigned for power during 1960. Lumumba won the national elections on May 11–25 and was sworn in as prime minister of a supposedly independent Congo on June 23. Kennedy won his election on November 8, 1960. However, whereas Nixon conceded defeat regretfully but gracefully, King Baudouin I of Belgium, chief opponent of independence, was extremely rude.

Baudouin saw Congolese independence as the climax of the Belgian civilizing mission. He said the Congolese should be grateful for the Belgian colonial genius; they should not change the structures the Belgians had set up for them, including those of his great-uncle, the mass murderer King Leopold II. Sole corporate owner of Congo Free State 1885–1908, Leopold II presided over the deaths of 10 million Congolese. Yet Baudouin chose the moment to tout that history as a good inheritance for Lumumba's Congo, a history to emulate.

Lumumba reminded the Congolese that, despite the round-table conferences in Brussels, their independence was not given to them but won by a day-to-day fight: "We are proud of this struggle, of tears, of fire, and of blood, to the depths of our being, for it was a noble and just struggle, and indispensable to put an end to the humiliating slavery which was imposed upon us by force."[20]

On January 17, 1961, six months after that statement, Lumumba was assassinated. Three days after, on January 20, Kennedy was sworn in as the head of the country whose CIA agents helped overthrow and murder Lumumba. The man who eventually took over the reins of power was the Belgium-sanctioned Joseph Mobutu. He immediately added Leopard to his name Mobutu. Leopard sounds like Leopold. Thus the Congo would move from the bloody arms of the foreign Leopold to the bloody claws of the native Leopard, both serving the same master—Western corporate and military interests.

The Congo Crisis—Moise Tshombe's secession, the death of Dag Hammarskjöld, Leopard Mobutu's military takeover, and the consequent fighting—became a centerpiece in the vocabulary of Cold War politics. The phrase "Congo chaos" was used as a cautionary metaphor against rapid decolonization by those who wanted to slow down the inevitable. But no force could slow down the MacMillan wind.

In Kenya it was a dog, a stone, and a Luger pistol that signaled that the wind had not bypassed the country. Many settlers placed a most feared sign on their gates: MBWA KALI, "fierce attack dogs." But some whites didn't even bother with the warning. Every settler's home had dogs trained to attack a black person. A favorite sport among settlers was setting dogs on Africans, then taking potshots at any who were running or simply sitting back to laugh at their frantic gestures of terror. But woe to any who might pick up stones or sticks to defend themselves! Bullets awaited them, for sure. Case closed. That had always been the ending of any story of blacks and whites and dogs until the day a dog, a pistol, and a stone collided in one Nairobi street.

The dog and the pistol belonged to Peter Poole, a soldier who had fought against the LFA and then set up an engineering shop on Government Road, Nairobi, now Moi Road. The stone belonged to Kamawe Musunge, Poole's houseworker, then called a houseboy. For reasons unknown, maybe for the usual sport, Peter Poole set two dogs on Musunge, who was riding a bicycle. We know Poole was the aggressor, for why else would the dogs attack, on their own, a person they had often seen in and about the house? Musunge, frightened, picked up a stone for self-defense. He didn't throw the stone, but Poole shot him dead for threatening his two attack dogs. The murder was barely news, and when, on October 12, 1959, Peter Poole was arrested, everybody, white and black alike, expected the case to go the way of the Kitosch story as told by Blixen in *Out of Africa*. However, the outcome was new and completely unexpected: the execution of Peter Poole on August 18, 1960, following his trial and conviction. In sixty years of corporate and colonial rule, after the deaths of countless Africans at the hands of gun-toting white settler cowboys, Peter Poole was the first and the only white person to hang for the crime. The name Peter means "rock," and Kamawe, the name of the man he killed for the crime of picking one up, also means "rock." Two rocks collided. Two men died. Two dogs survived.

The white uproar turned into a paroxysm of rage when in August 1961, Kenyatta was released from prison and assumed the leadership of the Kenya African National Union.

On December 9, 1961, Tanganyika became an independent

state with Mwalimu Julius Nyerere as prime minister. Mwalimu, an honorific meaning "teacher," shows how much the teacher was valued in the community. Nyerere was an old Makererean. On October 9, 1962, it was Uganda's turn, with Milton Obote as prime minister. Obote also was an old Makererean.

For those of us on the Hill at the time, Wordsworth better sums up the moment: "Bliss was it in that dawn to be alive, / But to be young was very heaven!"[21]

VII

We were young! Peter Kĩnyanjui, then president of the Makerere Students Dramatic Society, sought to celebrate the bliss with something more than drink, dance, and speech. We cannot share the moment with Shakespeare, he told me, referring to our previous roles in *Macbeth* in African robes, he as an actor and I as an assistant director.

Kĩnyanjui had graduated from Alliance a year after me, but even there he stood out as a great actor in Shakespeare's plays and in their modern counterparts. At Makerere, he played a brilliant Brother Jero in the eponymous play by Wole Soyinka.

"So?" I asked him.

"See the writing on the wall," he said. "Wanted! A three-act play. Help us make a dramatic point with your penpoint," he added, for emphasis.

I had never dreamed of anything more than a one-act drama. And now Kĩnyanjui was asking for a play with which to mark and celebrate Uganda's independence. In the wake of the triumph and disaster over *The Wound in the Heart*, the chance request presented an opportunity and a challenge. Seize the time; seize the day.

I said, "Only on one condition: that we perform it at the Kampala National Theater."

"A deal," he said. The society would look into the matter of venue; I, into the matter of script.

5

Penpoints and Fig Trees

I

Sixteen years later, at the Kamĩtĩ Maximum Security Prison, in which I was held as punishment for my community theater activities at Kamĩrĩthũ in Kenya, I looked back to that day in 1962, when, with only two small one-acts in my drama writing kit, I accepted Kĩnyanjui's challenge. I wondered, was it also the moment the writer in me was conceived?

Or did the miraculous conception begin years earlier in the evenings at my mother's hut where I first heard her stories of Swallow, who carried messages of those in distress; Hare, who fooled the biggies, Hyena, Lion, and Leopard, even arbitrating among them; Donkey, who brayed sorrow and shat mountains at the same time but also was so stubborn; and the scary two-mouthed ogre who lured beautiful maidens into his lair up in baobab and sycamore trees?

Or maybe it was a bit later, when I learned to read and I lost myself among the biblical characters of Abraham, Cain, Abel, Isaac, Rachel and Leah, Goliath and David, his sling not too dissimilar to the one I used to scare away the hawk who swooped down from the sky and snatched chicks from a mother hen or meat from the hands of a baby? Was it when I was held captive by David's harp strings, which time and again calmed the unpredictable tempests in the soul of King Saul? Maybe it started when I was first struck by the wonder that chalk marks on blackboards and pencil marks on paper could conjure up images that carried the combined power of the sling and the string.

Sometimes I think it came from a stint with Jim Hawkins on the high seas hunting for treasure on tiny islands in the Pacific or from escapes with Oliver Twist in the London streets of begging and hunger. I was continually amazed that I could travel to lands and seas far away and long ago while squarely ensconced in my Limuru rural outpost, thus attesting to the truth of the words that my classmate Kenneth Mbũgua and I recited to each other: Everyman, I will go with thee and be thy guide, in thy most need to go by thy side. We found these words in the Dent editions of Everyman's Library. Kenneth and I made the saying our own. We argued endlessly about the meaning of the phrase "every man," whether it actually meant everyone, including women and children.

Or maybe it happened at the house of my maternal grandfather, Ngũgĩ wa Gĩkonyo. I was named after him, and at times my mother would playfully call me her father. My grandfather had turned me into his scribe, writing his letters, and he would make me read them over and over again until I had gotten the tone, words, and imagery right.

At other times, I think it all began at Alliance High, where, without a Kenneth to argue with about phrases and the license to write, I first beheld Peter Abrahams's *Tell Freedom*, read

Brontë's *Wuthering Heights*, and dwelt in Tolstoy's *Youth*. Maybe I was conceived in the pages of Brontë and Tolstoy.

There had been other moments. There was the improvised drama in my village, with help from some Alliance boys, a dramatic mix of Christmas carols and freedom spirituals at Kamandūra Church. There was a similar mix at Kahūgūinī, where I was a temporary teacher. But those moments, though I was responding to the communal call and need, had not involved a written response to a challenge.

Or was it the day I took the Makerere Oath in July 1959, a gown with the color of blood hanging from my shoulders, and committed myself to a life of quest?

But there was indeed another day, I remember, when I faced a writing challenge: I was in my first year at Makerere when one of the English honors students stopped me in Queen's Court. "You must be the James Ngũgĩ we've been hearing about," he said.

He knew me? Heard about me? Me, a first-year? It was the first time I was hearing about my essays being read by anybody.

"My name is Jonathan Kariara," he added, and then told me that Peter Dane had read one of my essays to the honors group as an example of how to write an academic paper, especially as to judicious use of citations, comparisons, and contrast to develop an argument.

Kariara was then in his last year at college and was one of the stars in creative writing, having published some poems and stories in *Penpoint*, the signature product of the Department of English at Makerere. In years to come, he would establish himself as an editor in the Kenya branch of Oxford University

Press, but he remained ever the stylist, as in the stories he wrote for *Penpoint*.

II

The inaugural issue came out in 1958 under the title *The Magazine of the English Department* through the initiative of Alan Warner, professor and chair. In the next issue, it became *Penpoint*, because a writer uses the point of a pen to make a point, the image Kĩnyanjui would later echo in his dramatic challenge to me. The founding editorial board was made up of three students—Michael Woolman, Michael Kaggwa, and Peter Nazareth—and one faculty adviser, Murray Carlin. In 1959, Peter Nazareth was the editor and Peter Dane the faculty adviser.

I was most amazed not that students edited the magazine but that they wrote all those beautiful stories, poems, essays, and plays. Among the pieces I most liked was a short fiction, "And This at Last," by John Nagenda. A journalist, a product of the modern colonial school, goes back to his village to interview an old man about his life. Cocooned in his modernity, the journalist is arrogant, condescending, and takes as a given that he can teach the old man a thing or two about modern ways. By the end of the interview, it is the journalist who weeps, realizing how little of life he knows. The journalist character, with his attitudes toward the village and his general artificiality, could have been any one of us at Makerere.

Penpoint reawakened the desire to write, which I once experienced at Alliance, momentarily, but I had not yet done anything about it. And here I was face-to-face with Jonathan Kariara, one of the magazine's luminaries!

III

I stood there in awe. I wanted to talk with him further, but I didn't know what say. Talk of one's mouth drying up! We went our different ways, I feeling that there was something, whatever it was, I should have said but didn't.

A few days later, I bumped into him outside the Main Hall. I couldn't pass up the opportunity. I blurted out the first words from my mouth.

"Excuse me, I have written a short story, would you care to look at it?"

"Yes, give it to me, anytime," he said without hesitation, and left. After a few steps, he stopped and looked back: "Do you have it with you?"

"Oh, I am putting on the finishing touches—tomorrow, perhaps."

"Take your time."

I should have said that I'd been thinking about writing rather than that I had started doing it; I had transformed a vague desire into a fact that had yet to be actualized. I must now produce the fact; otherwise, how would I face him the next time?

I went back to my room in Northcote and immediately began the draft of my first short story, "The Fig Tree." It's the story of a woman in a polygamous household, a victim of domestic violence. She is childless; this would seem to be the problem between husband and wife. My character cannot take it anymore, and she decides to leave him. I was able to capture the senseless violence I had seen in my father's house against my mother, years ago. I wrote feverishly. I had not realized that I still carried the heaviness of the past. It was a relief when it all came out.

Kariara read the draft, returned it, and praised the quality of the writing but also talked about the difference between an episode and a story. I had merely described an event. "You cannot simply say, 'I went to Nairobi and back.' What happened there and why? Did the experience change the character in any way, even a small way?" He talked of irony, change, the invisible logic behind fiction where nothing happens by chance or coincidence. "The woman is beaten. She runs away. So what?"

I went back and worked on it, not one draft, but several. The woman still runs away, but finds refuge under the mũgumo, a sacred fig tree, where she seems to undergo some kind of spiritual experience, but in reality she simply realizes that she's already pregnant. Does she go away for good? But where to in a society where life is lived in close communion with the land and the community? Return? Given the new life she carries in her, she opts to return, hoping that this time the marriage will work.

Though the story and the domestic violence are based on my experience at home, there are important departures from the biographical. My mother had children, six in all, and when she finally left my father and went back to her father's place, she never returned. The fictional resolution of the conflict is not satisfactory, for it is not clear that anything has changed on the part of the man, but I put a lot into the evocation of the land, the spiritual transformation, and a sense of self, implying

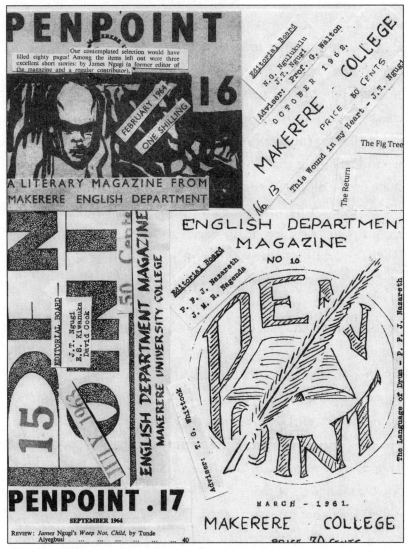

Penpoint collage by Barbara Caldwell from copies of *Penpoint*

that the woman's self-knowledge may make her assert herself more in the relationship.

"The Fig Tree" appeared in *Penpoint* number 5, December 1960, my first published work of fiction outside of "I Try Witchcraft," which had appeared in the Alliance High School magazine. I continued publishing stories in *Penpoint*, six in all, enough for me to have looked into their possible publication in book form.

A reference letter that my personal tutor, Mr. B.S. Hoyle, wrote on November 13, 1961, at the beginning of the first term in my first year in the English honors program, mentions this attempt. Noting that I was not a sportsman, that "his enunciation of English is not too good," but that my essays were always interesting to read, Hoyle also emphasized that I had spent my spare time writing stories and other contributions to *Penpoint*, adding, "He is endeavoring to arrange the publication of a selection of short stories he has written."

I had in fact sent all my short stories, including the juvenilia from Alliance, to some publishing houses, including Jonathan Cape, which rejected them. However, the reply from Hutchinson in London added that if I ever wrote a novel, the editors hoped that I would show it to them. Looking back, I knew I would be grateful forever that they had rejected the volume, because the uneven mix of the mature and the juvenile would have been a very unfortunate introduction to the world of books and book people.

But I was happy someone had made reference to a novel I might write. As 1960 turned into 1961, I embarked on a journey full of twists and turns, a literary awakening, which would impact my life profoundly.

6

Writing for the Money of It

I

The motive for the new venture was the announcement of a novel-writing competition open to all East Africans with a prize of one thousand shillings, equivalent to fifty British pounds at the time, to be administered by the East African Literature Bureau. The bureau was set up in 1947 by the British High Commission that regulated the interterritorial institutions of Kenya, Uganda, and Tanganyika. It published a lot of books in African languages, mainly school readers. The books were shorn of politics and issues that questioned the colonial order, but the bureau was important in making texts and readers available in African languages. The competition, funded by the Rockefeller Foundation, was the bureau's first project that went outside its norm and tradition.

It was Joe Mũtiga, a resident of New Hall next door, a budding poet, and a fellow contributor to *Penpoint*, who lit the flames of my ambition. New Hall may have been spoken of as a colony of Northcote, but when Mũtiga came to me, it was as a discoverer letting an ignorant native know that there was a world beyond the Makerere of the English Department,

Penpoint, and interhall rivalries. In that world, there were fortunes to be made and glories to be won. Lady Fortune, who ruled that world, didn't care if her supplicants were faculty or students, black or white, just so they were brave and daring. Let's dare, he challenged. I didn't need the challenge to motivate me: a thousand shillings in the pocket of a poor colonial student was beckoning me at the horizon. I fantasized the many things I would do with the unbelievable fortune.

II

I am in a dream. While others may be in it for literary glory, I am in it for gold, literally. But where do I start prospecting? Write about what?

The writers I have read for my English classes roll out in my mind: Charles Dickens, Jane Austen, Emily Brontë, George Eliot, Thomas Hardy, D.H. Lawrence. Can I follow in their footsteps? I have memories of my old favorite, Stevenson, who wrote of adventures in search of treasures.

But then I have recently come across Chinua Achebe's novel *Things Fall Apart* and Cyprian Ekwensi's *People of the City*. These two have dared: they have seen print. Did they also write for money?

There is Peter Abrahams also; his world of black and white in conflict is closer to mine in Kenya. Besides, he is not a stranger. I know he was friends with Jomo Kenyatta, Kwame Nkrumah, W.E.B. Du Bois. They were together at the Fifth Pan-African Congress in Manchester, England, in 1945, the turning point in anticolonial resistance. The others returned home—Kenyatta to Kenya to be jailed as a Mau Mau leader, at this time still languishing in prison; Nkrumah to be jailed as an agitator and then emerge from prison to become prime minister; and Du Bois to the United States to be tried as an enemy agent for his socialism and peace activism, his passport confiscated even though the charges were dismissed. Abrahams, the exile, driven from the South Africa he loved, well, he remained in England, trying to follow in the footsteps of Shakespeare. He went on to write for *The Observer*, sketches that later became *Return to Goli*, an account of a visit to South Africa. This man can write: *Paths of Thunder*, *A Wreath for Udomo*, and *Tell Freedom*. The last title mesmerized me at Alliance when I first beheld it in the hands of Allan Ogot, but I have rediscovered it in the Makerere library. Peter Abrahams always dreamed of becoming a professional writer. He wrote for money.

And then I have just read George Lamming's *In the Castle of My Skin*. A history teacher, Cheryl Gertzel, has let me delve into her home library. Lamming is from Babardos. How can this be, a Caribbean world speaking to me in ways so compelling that I want to do the same thing? Write about a village in Kenya. Write about Limuru. Write about my going to school under a hail of bullets. Write about life in an endless nightmare. Write about a community awakening to new life.

Easier thought than done. Nothing forms in my mind. No story. My Limuru and Kenya remain a land from which I have escaped, but I want to write about it; I want to make sense of it. I want to write about the women who are arrested and taken to the Home Guard post, who, when they come back, are silent about what happened. One can see that they are no longer the same, but they don't talk about it. There are only few whispers here and there, and sometimes one or two who are so crazed by the experience that they talk—of torture, bottles into their vaginas—but they don't give details. Only in their crazed state can they admit it in public. Men too, sodomized with bottles; some, their testicles crushed, nor can they talk about it, except when the "craziness" overtakes them.

I scribble a few words here and there, but nothing forms. I am upset. I have lived in the landscape of fear,[1] but I am unable to write about it. I know terror, but I can find no words to express it. I have seen villages razed, but I cannot find the image to capture the desolation. I seem helpless in the face of a reality that I have lived, that is still being lived by thousands in concentration camps and villages. How can the word fail me in my hour of need?

But Joe Mũtiga is writing; he reads me bits and pieces of what seems to be a folktale, but mostly he tells me the story. When I raise concerns, he says they didn't say that a fable couldn't be a novel. He is so confident; I can already see him, the happy supplicant, on whom Lady Fortune will surely smile. But I want her to smile on me, too, and Joe is so encouraging. This is strange, because I am the one who has already written and published a story, "The Fig Tree," and he's talking to me as though he has been there before, a literary veteran.

And then one night I hear a melody, then the words. In daytime, it follows me across the yard dividing Northcote and New Hall, up the path by the library, past the Main Hall, and into my classes in Queen's Court. It haunts me. I sing it, or rather, it sings in my mind, the melody and the lyrics.

My father my mother
If these were the days of our ancestors

I would ask you for cows and goats
Now I ask you to send me to school

My father my mother
Yesterday's heroes called for spears to defend the nation
Today's heroes demand pen and slate to save the nation
That's why I ask you to send me to school

We used to sing the song or variations of it in Manguo in the early 1950s, before the school, one of the many independently built and run by Africans, was shut down by the colonial state and reopened as a government-controlled institution.[2] The state banned the songs because they talked about the struggle for land, freedom, and education. I am aware that the ban is still in place, but I am in Uganda, a protectorate, a colony with no visible gun-toting settlers. Not that there's absolute safety anywhere for me, a member of the Gĩkũyũ, Embu, and Meru communities. It has not happened to me; no white man has stopped me on the streets of Kampala demanding to see my ID, but I know that early in 1952, teams of screeners had visited Makerere to ferret out any students already infected by the "Mau Mau." Some of them were disappeared; others lost their places. But that was then, not recently. In Kenya, the songs can still get me into trouble, but even there no power can stop a melody in the mind. The lyrics come back to me, subversive music from the underground—or is it from history? It's a history the colony tries to bury in a heap of white-skinned lies. My imagination digs up the history. It's a living history.

So memories come back: the daily walk to my primary schools, miles away; teachers dressed no better than some of the students, also walking to and from school, except the lucky one who possessed an old bicycle; buildings with leaking roofs; landowners like Kieya giving up portions of their land so that a school for the common good can be built; and yes, ordinary men and the women digging deep into their pockets, donating chickens, goats, cows, anything to come up with wages for the teachers or money needed to put up new buildings or buy material for desks. In some schools, the students make the desks and chairs as part of the classes in carpentry. A collective sacrifice to create our space for school.

Corfield denigrated this. Corfield scorned this. Corfield just consigned these people to the realm of the tree and the beast. African people contributed the major part toward the state treasury by way of poll or hut taxes; the colonial government spent the major portion of the treasury to beef up schools for the Europeans. African taxes built and maintained those schools; then the same Africans resorted to self-help and self-reliance to build their own schools. It was a double sacrifice: for European welfare and then their own survival. The Independent Schools Movement produced the first-ever teachers college in Kenya—Gĩthũngũri. Oh, Gĩthũngũri, now turned into a gallows center, a slaughterhouse of those who built it! But the dream?

Then it hits me—the dedication, the collective will. That's what I want to write about. The collective mania for education, the collective dreams for a meaningful tomorrow—I want to tell how it all began, that struggle for school. The barefoot teacher was at the center of the dream. He is the interpreter of the world; he brings the world to the people; he is the prophet of a tomorrow. I want to write about this so bad, it's like a fever that has seized me again and intensified. An outline of a teacher character begins to form in my mind. He takes on a name, Waiyaki. How? Why this among hundreds of possible names? But Waiyaki is not just any name; it resonates among Agĩkũyũ. It is the name of a legend. It is the name of history.

Waiyaki made a blood peace pact with Frederick Lugard, an agent of the Imperial British East Africa Company, on October 11, 1890. The Agĩkũyũ would supply the British caravans with food—fair trade. But Lugard and those who followed him, Eric Smith and William J. Purkiss in particular, had other ideas, and peace was not among them. They wanted armed pacification, white conquest for white settlement. Fort Smith was built in Dagoretti for that purpose. Waiyaki and his men stormed the citadel. Eventually Waiyaki was wounded and captured. He was marched to the coast. He died and was buried at a place called Kibwezi. Legend says he was buried alive, upside down, head pointing toward the bowels of the earth. His death taught us what it meant to desire land, freedom, and education.

My fictional Waiyaki is not the same historical figure. He is teacher, but a kind of avatar of the first, only that for a spear he holds a pen. The pen is mightier than the sword, they say. I borrow the name for my fictional character as a tribute to the historical Waiyaki. And the name takes me back to an earlier phase of Kenyan history: to understand the present, my present, I must first face the past, my past. The present is born of the power plays of the past.

Land, freedom, and education were the main themes in the politics that followed Waiyaki's defeat and the European and missionary settlement. Then the question of female circumcision became a battlefield of politics. In the 1920s, the missionaries, who now controlled African education, decreed that no student would be admitted into their schools unless the parents denounced the practice. Teachers, too, had to denounce it. Moreover, students, teachers, and their parents had to sign papers, *kĩrore*, affirming that they would never be members of nationalist organizations, like those led by Harry Thuku and Jomo Kenyatta after him, only of missionary- and state-approved associations. This insistence let people know that the real target was not the rite of passage[3] but anticolonial nationalism.

I think about the rite. It was one of many rites of passage in a society where legal, administrative, and political life was based on an age system. Circumcision was the boundary a person had to cross from childhood to adulthood. It determined the allocation of duties, responsibilities, and accountability.

But there's nothing sacred about any particular custom. Customs and practices that go with it change in the light of new knowledge. The Jews used to sacrifice human beings, but the story of Abraham and Isaac tells us there came a time when they substituted animal for human sacrifice. Many other societies have gone the same way. I have problems with customs that have outlived their initial basis of being.

Later in a newspaper column, I would describe the practice as brutal, a custom that African societies could well do without, and added that "it must be attacked mercilessly from all sides." This must have represented my thinking at the time, but I was also clear, on looking back to the political and cultural clashes over the issue, that it is wrong to use legitimate medical concerns to suppress legitimate political demands. Separate the two, then educate, but do not use a campaign against an oppressive rite to achieve an oppressive political agenda. But I have not figured this out yet; I want to explore it. Let's have a female character who is a victim of the rite. This is the starting point of my fictional exploration.

Another outline of a character emerges. She comes to me as an image from the past. I was in school at Manguo; she was the girl I was trying to impress when I once jumped over a barbed-wire fence, trying to fly over it with the insouciance of a champion. I fell and hurt my leg; she glanced in my direction briefly and went away. But the look, the enigma between amusement, arrogance, and puzzlement, stayed with me long after I had forgotten her physical features and my pain. The silhouette acquires a name: Mūthoni, in-law, the shy one who knows herself, the one who looks with detachment, pride, and a desire to know why. I don't know which is which, but the character intrigues me.

Mūthoni demands a sister, her opposite, the one who conforms rather than confronting, but they love and care for each other. Her silhouette emerges in the shape of a name, Nyambura, she who brings rain. She is one of the nine daughters of the legendary founders of the Agīkūyū.

Her other name is Mwīthaga, mother of the Ethaga clan, but Nyambura who brings rain sounds more right as the older sister of Mūthoni, the shy one.

It's also the name of a living Nyambura. Her father, Kīmunya, is the second son of her grandfather, Mūkoma wa Njiriri, the subject of nationalist lore. A colonial-appointed chief, Mūkoma was stripped of the dubious honor of being

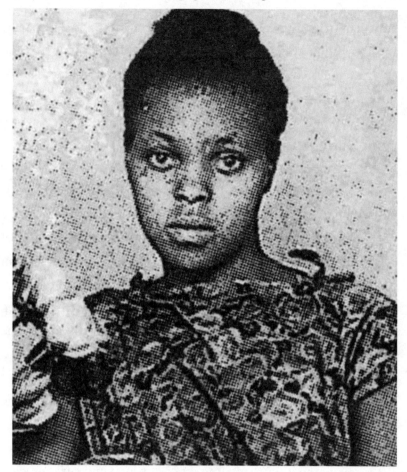

Nyambura, 1960

a colonial chief for leading an anticolonial resistance to the British takeover of the lands around Tigoni, *Ithaka cia Kanyawa*, for a white soldier settlement. His houses were among those torched by colonial police. He and others were forced to move to Ndeiya, but people never forgot his courage and defiance, and he became the subject of songs. Some of the songs ironically compared Mũkoma to Kĩnyanjui, the heroic chief of Karen Blixen's memoirs but a loathsome figure of nationalist memory, asking sarcastically which of the two was greater:

Mūkoma son of Njiriri
And Kīnyanjui son of Gathirimū
Who of the two is the greater leader
It has to be Kīnyanjui
He does whatever the whites tell him

Nyambura being the eldest daughter of Kīmunya, the son of Mūkoma would have been named after her paternal grandmother; from all sides the name belongs to legends.

I am three years older than she, but Nyambura and I grew up within a mile or so of each other; we had the same childhood friends; went to the same schools, Kamandūra and then Kīnyogori. I continued into high school; she did not. But the more our paths parted, the more rapidly our hearts drifted toward each other, and by the time I went to Makerere in 1959, we had entered into a soul pact we always knew was coming.

The living on earth and the living on a page merge into a living image; they share the name and the quality of making rainfall. From as far as my memory went, rain had been part of it. We always welcomed it with lyric variations of the same melody:

Rain pour on
I offer you a calf for sacrifice
One and another
With bells around the neck
Ding-dong-ding-dong[4]

Nyambura is mythic and historical, whereas Waiyaki is historical and mythic. Nyambura and Mūthoni demand a father.

Joshua is an amalgam of the various fire-and-brimstone Protestant preachers I knew.

And suddenly, out of the four-legged stool of Joshua,
Nyambura, Mũthoni, and Waiyaki, a story of struggle over
the soul of the land emerges. I set it in the space of the early
European colonial ventures into the interior. It's a time before
I was born, but it feels very right. I can even see the landscape;
it has all the features of the one I once beheld in Mũrang'a on
my way to Nyeri to honor Baden Powell—the land of sleeping
lions on either side of the Thagana River, lions with the potential of roaring to life. I see everything in the mist of time, and
it ignites my imagination.

I am trembling inside. I jot a few lines, but the trembling
won't stop. I so badly want to see everything in all its clarity,
but the mist hides the sharp edges of the connections yet also
makes them more alluring. Like magic. It is magic. Imagination is the magic that makes possible connections across time
and space.

Years later, Dinwiddy would tell the story of how one evening I knocked at the door of their house, my demeanor serious, my face concerned. He invited me in and, thinking it an
emergency, took me aside to the veranda, away from the piano-
playing Yvonne, to hear me out in private.

"I am afraid I have started writing a novel," I blurted out,
trusting he would understand.

Actually I had written to him a shy note earlier telling him
about my literary intent, and I may have turned to him, despite
the awkward hour, because I assumed he already knew. In the
course of writing it, I went to him at many awkward hours,
but he didn't complain.

But that first time was important. I don't remember the exact words. He offered me fruit juice, maybe hoping to coax out the real reason of my visit, but I didn't add another word to the confession. I felt a little foolish. He looked bemused. Writing a novel was not such a bad idea, he assured me, and once done, I could always show it to him. "Do you have a title?" he asked.

"Yes, 'Wrestling with God.'"

III

It's a working title. It comes from Genesis 32:24–26 (quoted here in the English Standard Version), where Jacob wrestles with an angel after he has safely seen his household across a stream at night.

> And Jacob was left alone. And a man wrestled with him until the breaking of the day. When the man saw that he did not prevail against Jacob, he touched his hip socket, and Jacob's hip was put out of joint as he wrestled with him. Then he said, "Let me go, for the day has broken." But Jacob said, "I will not let you go unless you bless me.

It's an unforgettable image of a human wrestling with a superhuman force. It has the somber but pleading balance of demand, deference, and defiance. It creates a certain mood in me, in harmony with my struggle in my room alone, trying to do something that has not been done in Makerere. Word has spread that Mũtiga and I are writing novels. The news evokes from my fellow students not admiration but sniggers of mockery, at least from some. "I understand you're writing a book, eh? You're barely into your second year, and you think you can do what even our professors can't do?"

It's as if they have already forgotten the Makerere oath. Hierarchy cannot stand in the way of the search for truth, at least in the commitment to it. Even a child can point out that the emperor has no clothes. Besides, others have done it, in ages past and different nations and regions. What one can do, another can also, I urge myself. These are words I once heard from one of my teachers in Manguo Elementary School. He used to say it more dramatically. What one man can do, another man can do. But I need the blessing of the muse.

Occasionally I get curious voices of genuine fascination with the possibility. Bethuel Kiplagat, whose room is next door, calls on me from time to time. He is always the encouraging prefect of our days at Alliance. He is a year ahead of me. His curiosity is always a shot in the arm.

For months on end throughout 1961, stealing moments from my other college commitments, I struggle with the novel. Suddenly one day I come to a block, and no amount of Jacob wrestling with the angel and pleading with the muse not to pass me by will make anything click. I'm stuck. The little voice of despair whispers soothingly, Why are you doing this, anyway? It isn't going to make you perform better or worse in the exams. You want an academic degree, not a literary pedigree. I succumb. I don't want to go on.

In my next meeting with Joe Mũtiga to discuss the Novelists' Progress, I report despair. Mũtiga is upbeat. He talks about the award. The haul of one thousand shillings! Keep your eye on the prize. He is great. We're competitors, and yet he's so encouraging. OK, I'll try. I will confront the block.

And the muse comes back. For a few more months, I ride on incredible waves of pure exhilaration, as the mists of time begin to clear. I go back to Mūtiga to report spectacular progress. Alas, *he* is now stuck. He wants to give up, claiming that he's satisfied with being a poet. No, I urge him, literally throwing his words back at him: keep your eye on the prize, the shine of notes worth a thousand shillings, some with King George's head, others with Queen Elizabeth's head. Imagine the wealth awaiting the victor. I keep at it for days, but he doesn't respond with "I'll try" or anything about riding on new waves of desire. No matter how hard I try, he will not clutch at the literary rope. I know it's hopeless, because he no longer seeks me out to show me his stuff or to know about mine. I feel lonelier than before.

The living Nyambura comes into the picture. She is expecting. I miss her. I want to be with her; our moments together whenever I go home for holidays are never long enough for me. But through my fictional Nyambura, I can feel the living presence of the other, who is also carrying another life. Of course, the fictional Nyambura is not modeled on the real one, who is just the inspiration, but the nominal resemblance, though fleeting, is enough to spur me on. Sometimes it's simply the thought of her smile at finding her name inhabited by a character in a book that adds to the call of the muse.

On September 10, Nyambura the living gives birth to our son Thiong'o, named after my father. From now on, I shall have two lives: a family man in Kenya, an academic man in

Makerere. The family will affect how I organize my academic and literary life: provide a focus, palpable reason, motive, and purpose for doing whatever I do with pen and paper.

Somehow I am able to plod through to some form of a draft. I give Dinwiddy the handwritten manuscript. The fact of showing somebody the completed draft of a novel, my first ever, makes me do something that I keep telling myself I should do but never do! Write a diary. The first entry has the date: November 3, 1961.

> Have decided to start a diary. Been toying with the idea for quite a long time. But tonight the idea forcibly came back after a glance of Somerset Maugham's writer's notebook. That was at Mr. Dinwiddy's house. We were sitting in his study. Full of books. His wife was playing the piano. Mr. Dinwiddy was discussing my first novel with me. I don't know why I feel guilty when I call it my novel. But it is. "The Black Messiah." Mr. Dinwiddy is kind. How can he take so much trouble? Sometimes I was not listening to what he said. His wife was playing the piano beautifully. I think I like piano music. Then she stopped. Silence. Went on discussing. . . .

He makes useful comments, something about telling it in images. Instead of saying that a character is tall and thin, why not more descriptive words like lanky and gangly? I can see he's trying hard not to overdisplay his emotions, but the bottom line—he likes it. I am happy.

At home in Kenya during the December holidays, when not hugging the new life, I find the time to work on the manuscript revisions in the light of Dinwiddy's comments. I have dared do something that has not been done in Kenya or East Africa: write a novel. I know, I know—there has been some fiction written by European writers who claim to be Kenyan. Elspeth Huxley leads the pack with such titles as *Murder at Government House* (1937), *The Red Strangers* (1938), and *A Thing to Love* (1954). Then there's the American, Robert Ruark, with his *Something of Value.* But they write about adventures of white heroes in Africa, with black people as decorative background along with fauna and flora.

But now I feel that I'm part of something in the air. It's not only the new reality in my life. Everywhere in the country, there's something that we have not seen in years. Hope. Optimism. We were making things happen; we were making history.

We now live in the post-Emergency era, martial law having been lifted in 1960. There is the glow from Kenyatta's release on August 21 and Tanzania's independence on December 9, 1961. I know the meaning of the glow: hope for a new dawn— for the country, for me as a writer. Hope for a future for the life that Nyambura has brought to earth. Hope for the birth of a new nation.

I am in time to meet the deadline. But I don't want to post the handwritten manuscript to the bureau. It's the only copy I have. Suppose it gets lost in the mail?

Accompanied by my younger brother, Njinjū, I take a bus to Nairobi and walk to the offices of the East African Literature

Njinjũ, Ngũgĩ's younger brother

Bureau, where on December 28, 1961, I deliver the manuscript. The title has morphed from "Wrestling with God" to "The Black Messiah," and years later it will be published as *The River Between*.

7

Black Dolls and Black Masks

I

I had thought, when I first arrived in the city, that living in Kampala, where blackness was the dominant visual norm, would ensure my final escape from the black-and-white consciousness that had defined my reality and history in a white-settler-dominated society. I soon realized that every black person must at some time discover his blackness in a twentieth-century world whose problem W.E.B. Du Bois once described as that of the color line. In Kenya we called it the color bar, the term entering African languages as variations of *karambaa*. "We reject color bar" was Jomo Kenyatta's clarion call when, in 1946, after fifteen years away, he returned to the country to lead the Kenya African Union (KAU)[1] in the struggle for land and freedom.

"Kenya was the land of black people," we sang in opposition to the European settlers' claims that Kenya was the White Highlands. Their claims had been given literary immortality in the work of Elspeth Huxley. The colonial state sided with the literary, but the oral was the voice of a people, and even after the state banned FLA songs and poetry, song and dance inspired defiance in those herded in barbed-wired trucks into concentration camps. They sang:

> *Deport us to concentration camps*
> *Or lock us up in prisons*
> *Or exile us on remote islands*
> *We shall never cease to struggle for freedom*
> *Kenya is the land of black people*[2]

The song expressed defiance and a collective discovery of blackness. But there was also a personal discovery of blackness, and sometimes one had to find it not once but several times.

II

My first discovery of blackness was not the time when as a child I saw Europeans in the streets or saw the road-building Italian prisoners of war in our villages buying eggs and seeking sex. Their color was clearly outside the norm, and those who once called the incomers *mzungu*, skinless spirits, may have looked at them with the unjudgmental eyes of children. A norm is not discovered; it is taken for granted, needing neither affirmation nor refutation. My first real discovery was when a young armed white officer, a machine gun slung from the shoulder, temporarily blinded me with a blow to my face and I could not respond in kind, as my manhood, newly earned by undergoing circumcision, would otherwise have made mandatory.[3]

The second was after graduating from high school, when I was incarcerated on the orders of a white officer hardly older or more schooled than me.[4] I saw grown men cower at his word, reminding me of King Lear's saying that even a dog is obeyed in office. White was the color of power. White would always checkmate black until black also expressed power. Black power was the only real answer to white power. Only then could a dialogue between equals emerge.

My third discovery of blackness came from my encounters with a whiteness different from the missionary type at Alliance, the bureaucratic and settler kind in the Kenyan streets and farmlands, or the cap-and-gown crowd at Makerere. It was a type that looked as if it lived out of time and out of place. One could not quite describe it; one had to have worked at the EAAFRO, acronym for East Africa Agriculture and Forestry Research Organization, to see and assess it.

The organization, stationed at Muguga, halfway between Nairobi and Limuru, off the Nairobi–Naivasha road, was the result of rival imperialisms with roots in the nineteenth-century Scramble for Africa. After the 1884 Berlin conference, the Germans ended up with Tanganyika and Mount Kilimanjaro. In 1902 they built a research station in the Amani region of the East Usambara Mountains. With the defeat of the Germans in World War I, Tanganyika changed hands. In 1928, the new colonial owners, the British, named the Amani institution the East African Agricultural Research Station and in 1948 moved it to Muguga, Kenya, to form the East African Agricultural and Forestry Research Organization (EAAFRO), mandated to meet the research needs common to the three British colonial possessions of Kenya, Tanzania, and Uganda.

I was driven there by the need for a job. The Makerere academic year had three breaks, during which students went home. At the height of the State of Emergency, some Kenyans sought to stay at Makerere with special permission. But with the formal end of the Emergency in 1960, we took every opportunity to go home. At first it felt good traveling back and forth in second-class rail coaches, but after the novelty wore off, we found the buses, though less comfortable, much quicker. If one had a job, the sooner one started on it, the better.

The wages from vacation jobs supplemented the meager student allowances, but the jobs were not easy to come by. One sent applications everywhere, and it was a lucky day when one got acknowledgment of the effort. So I felt blessed when, early in my first year, I was called to EAAFRO to work in its library division.

The station was about thirteen miles from Limuru, and often I went there on foot. But even when I was lucky and got into the buses of uncertain regularity, I still had to walk the last two miles off the main Naivasha–Nairobi road to the station, hidden deep in the forest.

At first it was a novelty: I looked forward to working for scientists, researchers, serious thinkers, people whose lives were dedicated to what the Makerere oath stood for: rigorous pursuit of truth. They were guided by facts, not fiction, and reason, not emotion.

Lady Viviana[5] was the head of the library division. Under her was a white deputy, Mrs. Smart Ogletree,[6] and under them, an African assistant, Moses Wainaina.[7] Moses was obsequiousness made flesh when it came to any of the white officers. In their presence, he would stand at attention, becoming visibly invisible, until they had passed or, in the case of Lady V. and Smart O., till they had completed their instructions. As they left, he became visibly visible slowly and surely in proportion to the distance between him and them. Moses was completely the opposite when it came to the staff under him. He expected them to be equally obsequious to him, and when they would not, he became intolerant, mistreated them and finally drove them out and got a new batch. Each time he would lecture them on the correct decorum when in front of white people, and if they didn't meet his standards in work or manners, he would feel that they were doing things slovenly in order to get him fired. He hated with equal fervor any who tried to endear themselves to Lady V. The turnover of the subordinate staff was high, making temporary jobs always available. Moses tolerated me because I came from Makerere and because I was there only for vacations, three weeks in most cases, except for the three-month break. I think he also liked it that a Makererean was working under him. One day he became very alarmed when he found out that I was going to the bathroom frequented by the whites. That one is for white people, he told me. But I replied that it wasn't written anywhere that it was whites-only.

The researchers had lived for so long in a world of test tubes, greenhouses, and viruses that they had come to think of their black underlings as some kind of plant or animal blight to be handled with gloved care. They reminded me of George Eliot's Casaubon, living with the dead while he looked for the keys to all mysteries.

Things were happening around them. MacMillan's wind was blowing across Africa, but these people seemed oblivious of history on the move. The Happy Valley—the interwar settler society of British aristocrats enjoying the lush life from the labor of blacks—was the only memory of Kenya's past they seemed to know and cherish, and they tried to emulate and replicate it. They would emerge out of their greenhouses and labs to savage each other over their spouses, the aggrieved parties chasing each other in cars or with guns drawn. Once three of them became entangled in a love triangle. They entered the annual East Africa safari-car rally that used to start at Nairobi, winding through dirt, mud, and rain across the three countries. Lady V. was the pilot to her lover in one car, her husband following behind in another. It turned out to be a race between the two cars, the husband trying to knock the other car off the road. Somehow, according to Moses, they survived, and the love triangle survived the race intact.

Lady V. was at the center of the Muguga replication of the Happy Valley. Moses regaled me with every salacious saga he had encountered. When she and one of her lovers locked themselves in her office, they didn't see him as a presence. Nevertheless, despite his apparent fear, Moses was wily enough to occasionally knock at the door innocently and enjoy the reaction of muffled voices or complete silence.

It was only when detailing such episodes that Moses smiled or laughed. It was as if they had allowed him to peep at the dirty secrets of their joy.

Otherwise Moses seemed afflicted by an anti-nationalism virus. He thought that all the talk about freedom and black rule was pure ignorance and stupidity. Black people were incompetent. Black people would ruin standards. He seemed genuinely terrified of the very possibility of black rule, and one of a new batch who knew him from home hinted that Moses may have acted as one of the hooded men who outed LFA suspects to execution or concentration camps.

For some reason, I never actually met anybody in the bathroom, and this seemed to relax Moses. But one day, during one of the vacations, I went to the bathroom, and as I came out, an officer, whom I later learned was the general administrative officer, happened to enter. At first he passed me but then suddenly stopped and looked back as if he couldn't believe what he had just seen. When I told Moses about the encounter, he became visibly shaken. For the rest of the day, he wouldn't speak to me. Every time Lady V. called him to the office, he would tremble all over: this was it, he was going to pay for my shitting ways. He relaxed only after it seemed he would not be held accountable. He begged me on his knees to please not jeopardize his career by visiting the white bathrooms. My position remained the same: it was not written that the bathrooms were segregated. I was being legalistic!

Another white officer who met me in the bathroom another time reacted with the same surprised incomprehension as the first. Eventually, Lady V. called me to her office. I was holding a book, *The Greeks*, by H.D.F. Kitto, in my hands. She first glanced and then asked to look at it, surprised that I was reading such a book, probably the first time it registered that I was a college student. She then tried to tell me that those bathroom facilities were for the officers only, that I could use the others. She didn't seem to know the location of the "others"; she just gestured vaguely. But those others were very far, I said, too few for too many people. Besides, there was no sign saying they were for white people. She corrected me: "No, no, officers."

She seemed embarrassed to be arguing about bathrooms, and I left it at that.

But the saga of two nails dwarfed that of the bathroom. It so happened that one day Lady V. asked me to run to the workshop and get her two nails. The workshop served the entire station. I had to walk across a quadrangle of grass to get there. The Indian carpenter would not part with two nails without written permission from the clerk of works, a white man. So I walked into his office. He was a fairly short man, very fond of hats; he had different hats for different clothes. Would he give me two nails for Lady V.? He growled at me: *kwenda leta barua*. What? Go back and get a letter? He couldn't trust me with two nails without a letter from my boss?

Lady V. picked up the phone, said something, and then duly gave me a chit. It was back to the clerk of works. He literally snatched the letter from my hands and then walked into the workshop, I following. All of a sudden, he turned around and roared at me: *toa mkono mfuko*. Take my hands out of my pockets? I refused. The man tried to take them out physically, forcefully. I had to restrain myself to avoid a physical altercation. I simply walked away without the nails. I reported the incident to Lady V. "I will see to it" was all she said, and I never heard about the matter again. Whatever her personal life was, Lady V. was actually very nice, and I never heard her utter racially offensive words, to my face, at least, but the signal was clear: it was time I left EAAFRO, vacation jobs or not.

A couple of weeks before I left the place for good, I saw a sign near the bathrooms: FOR OFFICERS ONLY. There was not a single African officer at the time.

Years later, the location and the people I encountered would appear a fictitious place and as characters in my novel *A Grain of Wheat*, and one reviewer in Canada who had lived in Kenya expected a libel suit against me. He claimed that anybody who had lived in the country at the time would recognize the real persons behind the mask of fiction.

It was during my EAAFRO period that I dreamed up various stories, among them "The Village Priest," "And the Rain Came Down," and "The Black Bird." These stories had nothing to do with EAAFRO directly, but the lone walk through the awesome singing silence of the thick forest set in motion images close to the sacred.

The stories were published in various issues of *Penpoint* and in other regional magazines, like *Nilotica*. Some, including "The Black Bird," were adapted for radio in 1962, along with the one-act drama *The Rebels*,[8] and broadcast by the Uganda Radio. Miles Lee, head of the Drama Department, with the help of the indefatigable David Cook, gave national forum to the literary production around *Penpoint*.

A mystery man, Miles Lee had a successful past freelancing for the BBC, fortune-telling at the Goose Fair in Nottingham, stage-directing for the Birmingham Repertory Theatre, and running his own company, the Belgravia Mews Puppet Theatre in Edinburgh. I never knew how he came to abandon his real love, puppetry, for radio in Uganda, because he hinted at it more than he spoke about it. He seemed uncomfortable at parties at Makerere but luxuriated in his own at Kololo Hill, an upscale residential neighborhood beloved of expatriates and civil servants. The white people who came to his party looked haunted, as if they were fugitives from wherever in the outposts of the British Empire they had once served. Though very different from the EAAFRO crowd, they all looked like figures lifted from the pages of Conrad, ex-dwellers in outer stations somewhere in the Congo or the Far East.

A goodly number of these had black mistresses or wives, and apart from Miles, who seemed deeply and genuinely in love with his wife, the others seemed to treat them as erotic toys for social display, almost a kind of proof that they had no race prejudice.

At one of his parties, I met the mustached Bob Astles, who, years later, would figure prominently as advisor to Idi Amin. An alleged British spy, he was first sent to Uganda in 1949 for "special duties." His droopy mustache, so ordinary that it almost stood out, was more impressive than his intellectual presence—hence my surprise at the role he later came to play in Uganda's fate.

III

My third discovery of blackness was literary. In an article in *Penpoint*, Gerald Moore introduced the poetry of the Négritude literary movement to Makerere. Cambridge educated and director of the Makerere Extra-Mural Department, Moore was then one of three European scholars, the others being Ulli Beier and Janheinz Jahn, who took a serious look at the emerging literature from the continent.

The three men were linked by their relationship to the work of Léopold Sédar Senghor from Senegal. Jahn met Senghor in Frankfurt in 1951, heard of black poetry for the first time, and became a student and translator of this new thing. In 1958, he published his own anthology of contemporary African and African-American poetry, *Black Orpheus*, the same title given by Jean-Paul Sartre to an essay originally published in 1948 as the preface to the *Anthologie de la nouvelle poésie negre et malgache de langue francaise*, edited by Senghor, one of the three founders of Négritude. Léon Damas, from then French Guiana, and Aimé Césaire, from Martinique, were the other two.

Ulli Beier first met Senghor in 1956 in Paris at the First World Congress of Black Writers and Artists. He was awestruck by the new work, and he became its student and translator. He founded the Nigeria-based journal *Black Orpheus* in 1961. Gerald Moore was also a translator of Senghor and the new African writing into English. Years later, he and Ulli Beier would put together an influential collection, *The Penguin Book of Modern African Poetry*,[9] with the poetry of Senghor and Négritude at the center of it.

I read and reread with astonishment the lyrical rendering of blackness, the music coming through even in Moore's translation.

> *Black mask, red mask, you black and white masks,*
> *Rectangular masks through whom the spirit breathes,*
> *I greet you in silence!*[10]

Likewise his address to the black woman:

> *Naked woman, black woman*

> *Clothed with your colour which is life,*
> *with your form which is beauty!*[11]

Reading the poetry of Négritude was like seeing my face in a mirror for the first time, whereas before I had seen only other faces reflected there. Theirs was a literary mirror of blackness as color, history, and active being. I recalled the arguments I'd had in school about black Jesus, the color of God, and here was a poetry affirming blackness as an active value and force in history.

In time, however, I started to react against the overemphasis on an undifferentiated blackness, principally in an article submitted in 1961 but published in *The Undergraduate* of May 1962 under the title "Give Me My Black Dolls: The African Dilemma." The title was taken from the fourth stanza of the poem "Borders," by Léon Damas:

> *Give me back my black dolls to play*
> *the simple games of my instincts*
> *to rest in the shadow of their laws*
> *to recover my courage*
> *my boldness*
> *to feel myself myself*
> *a new self from the one I was yesterday*
> *yesterday*
> *without complications*
> *yesterday*
> *when the hour of uprooting came.*[12]

I critiqued the nostalgia, what I then saw as an uncritical longing for a past that would never come back, ending the article with a call for some kind of synthesis of the positive elements from the three ways of life in East Africa—Asian, European, and African. I am not sure how different this was from Senghor's call for a similar synthesis of what, years later, Ali Mazrui, following Edward Blyden and Kwame Nkrumah, would call "the triple heritage." With time, I have come to admire the literature of Négritude, recognizing that it had a variety of voices. Reacting to the few poems that came through then, I had sinned in seeing it as uniform.

An adaptation of the article, a critique of Négritude, was my first piece of cultural journalism, appearing in the May 12, 1961, issue of the now defunct *Sunday Post*. I cited Wole Soyinka's famous quip about the tiger not needing to roar its tigritude. Soyinka had, of course, added the positive: it pounces.

IV

Frustration with EAAFRO had made me look to the pen for an alternative source of extra cash. But I also felt that I was developing ideas beyond those demanded by my class papers, ones that I could not readily translate into fiction. I had a viewpoint, the language to express it, and the energy to sustain the effort.

I published a few more pieces in the *Sunday Post*, on cultural themes, mainly, while also working on "The Black Messiah" for the competition. Though they didn't change the content of my articles, the editors would sometimes give them headlines that didn't reflect the content and form of the article. I soon learned that writers of stories and features in newspapers had no control over the headline and subheadings. An editorial frame could at times clash with the content and intent of one's piece.

Publication emboldened me to try for an actual job at a newspaper office. During one vacation in the second half of my first year at college, I walked into the offices of the *Sunday Post* and sought to see the editor. It was then an all-white office, and I don't know what kind of figure I struck, but the receptionist took my name, and after a while, I was led into the editor's office.

He introduced himself as Jack Ensoll and offered me a seat on the opposite side of a huge mahogany table. I noticed little else, so nervous I was, but in the friendly manner of his reception, I read, "You've got a job." He knew my name, from the note the receptionist had scribbled or maybe from my contribution, probably the first African they had ever published. He went through the preliminaries. What was I doing, how was I doing it? I thought that my being in my second year at college would work against me, so I kept on assuring him that all I wanted was a vacation job. He wanted to know what I wanted to do after college. My eventual goal was to become a journalist.

As we talked, he dialed somebody, and soon the newspaper that contained one of my articles was spread before him. I was sure of a deal.

"I want to tell you my honest opinion," Jack said. "I have read and liked your articles. I like the way you write, how you use words, but a few months in this desk, and it's all gone, the individual voice, the something you have. Please don't let us ruin what you have. Your future lies between hard covers."

He wished me all the best as he led me to the door. It was all polite, but what I then most needed was a job, not a future in hardcovers.

I turned to the *Sunday Nation*. The paper and its sisters, the *Daily Nation* and *Taifa Leo*, were publications of East African Newspapers (Nation series) Ltd., later the Nation Media Group, owned by the Aga Khan. Established between 1958 and 1960, they were the newest kids on the block, competing with the oldest newspaper in the country, the *East African Standard*, which Alibhai Mulla Jeevanjee had started in 1902 but sold in 1905 to British businessmen, who turned it into a daily. The old, aligned with white-settler interests, was no match for the new, aligned with inclusive change. Their very titles, *Nation* and *Taifa*,[13] looked to a life after the colony. Soon after, the *Sunday Post* went out of business for good. The *Sunday Nation* reigned supreme on Sundays.

V

My first article in the *Sunday Nation* appeared in May 1962. A few more, and they gave me a regular column, under the title As I See It, bylined James Ngugi.

Writing a weekly column was a challenge. I had no background in journalism. I was used to writing academic papers for class, but I soon came to sense the difference between the footnoted academic paper, with numerous citations and references, and the journalistic essay aimed at a mass audience. I learned to make only one point, in a structure of beginning, middle, and end, but the subject or theme had to come right at the beginning.

Initially, getting a different subject for each Sunday was equally challenging. But I came to learn how to pick my subject from the general news during the week. Mine really was opinion journalism, and it had parasitic relations to the news gathered and written by others in the dailies. But I also dug into my literary heritage, writing, in a popular form, what I encountered in my studies as an English honors student. So the names of writers and books that I read in or outside the classroom would find their way into some of the write-ups.

Having to rely on my take on some aspect of current news also meant developing a personal view on what was unfolding in Kenya and Uganda, and sometimes in Africa and the rest of the world. I had not formed a comprehensive worldview, but I grew up in a race-structured society where white was wealth, power, and privilege and black was poverty, impotence, and burden, where white was indolence and black was diligence, a society where whites harvested what blacks planted. This dichotomy gave me a frame through which I saw the world. Amid contradictions, incoherence, and half-formed opinions, I came to develop themes that would later find their way into my fiction and nonfiction, particularly the issues raised by inequalities of power and wealth in society.

In fact, concerns over the social conditions of the ordinary working man and woman were to be found in many of my articles, alongside those that focused on education, pan-Africanism, freedom of the press, and suspicions about extremism. Most consistent was my belief in art and literature and theater as being central in the emerging new Africa. In the case of theater, I even called on the Makerere College Dramatic Society to organize a touring company. Twelve months after the article was printed, faculty and students launched the Makerere Travelling Theatre.

If there is any overarching theme in my articles of the Makerere period, it would be humanism, with art and culture occupying a venerable place. To me, humanism implies real human care. Thus the As I See It column in the *Sunday Nation* of September 9, 1962, was titled "What About Our Neighbors?" I focused on the plight of beggars as the neighbor we meet in the streets but don't want to acknowledge. This helped me raise the question of social mutual care: I looked forward to a time when "Kenya will be in a position to cater for the economic and social welfare of all her citizens," but also cautioned that "a social welfare state cannot be built on begging abroad—a thing which every newly independent country is forced to do."

In another column, on April 14, 1963, I commended the East African Literature Bureau for producing books in vernaculars. In so doing, I argued, the bureau "not only helped the children, who would otherwise have had to depend on translations alone, but has helped those African authors writing in the vernacular."

Time and again, I came back to the language question. While I appreciated English, I was also concerned about the place of the other languages, particularly Kiswahili.

For instance, in the *Sunday Nation* of September 23, 1962, under the heading, "Swahili Must Have Its Rightful Place," I started by lamenting the fact that African writers were "forced to tame the music and strifes in their own souls by having to use a foreign language. This was not because the African languages were necessarily inferior to French or English but because "the study of vernacular languages especially in secondary schools and colleges has been totally neglected." This neglect of indigenous languages remained "a black spot in the whole of colonial education in Africa." I challenged writers in general and African writers in particular to produce more work in these languages to ensure enough material for reading and study, concluding, "I do not think for a moment that we can ever be a nation of any importance unless we have a language of our own through which our national aspirations and spiritual growth can be expressed."

While I applauded African culture and its centrality in emergent Africa, I also warned against an uncritical worship of the past. In the *Sunday Nation* of August 5, 1962, under the title "Let Us Be Careful About What We Take from the Past," I wrote strongly against two customs: bride-price and female circumcision. I argued that the two had outlived their purpose and original rationale. Bride-price, dowry as it is sometimes called, had been turned from a kind of marriage insurance, as in the past, "into a profitable commercial enterprise." I was harsher on female circumcision, which I said is "brutal and shows a callousness to human suffering. It is quite nauseating to see some obviously very young girls being subjected to this, even on the verge of independence." I took issue with some who called themselves enlightened and yet "condone the custom, who make the ordinary man feel that it has something special to do with his culture or with the more mystical African personality." I called upon leaders of opinion to come out in the open and condemn this with one voice: "It must be attacked mercilessly from all sides."

In time I built a following in Kenya and, closer home, among my fellow students. But theirs was more of a general admiration that I wrote a regular column in a national newspaper than a critical engagement with what I wrote. The exception was J. Njoroge. He thought I was selling out to a

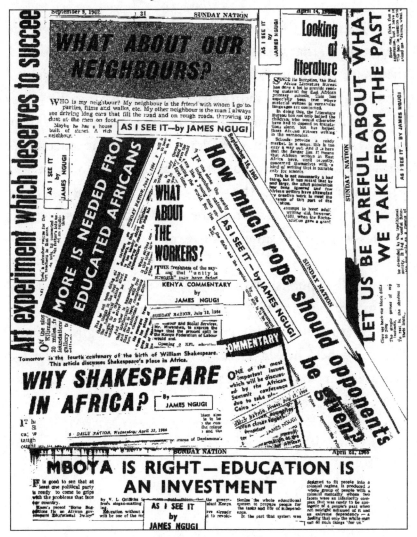

A collage by Barbara Caldwell of *As I See It* and *Commentary* articles
from *Sunday Nation/Daily Nation* written by Ngũgĩ

newspaper owned by the Aga Khan. To my rejoinder that they
never interfered with pieces, that they never dictated what I
say or any of my opinions, he countered by saying there was
no such a thing as a completely independent journalism, that
one wrote within the general consensus of a newspaper. A

newspaper had a world outlook and journalists worked within that outlook, that if they tried to go outside, they would find themselves without a job. He would have preferred I stick to creative writing. But I didn't abandon my journalism.

In the five years of my stay at Makerere, I wrote more than eighty essays, mostly under As I See It, but also as general features in the Nation Group of newspapers and in other newspapers and magazines. The weekly retreat into the streets was obviously good catharsis from the world of textbooks, because my classwork didn't suffer at all, except for a few papers handed in late.

Journalism published in newspapers was my first major foray into writing. However, when later I got an invitation to the First International Conference of Writers of English Expression to be held in Makerere in June 1962, it was clearly not because of my journalism but my then modest literary output.

8

Transition *and That Letter from Paris*

I

I could hardly believe it. I'm a second-year college student, and I'm being invited to a gathering of literary giants? The letter even suggested that one of my works, "The Return," would be discussed in the short-story session.

"The Return" tells the story of a man who comes home from a concentration camp looking forward to resuming life where he left it at the time of his arrest. It seemed to him that life must have stood still waiting for his return. But even in his absence life has flowed on. History rolls on; people have moved on; things can never be the way he imagined they would be. At first he feels let down, as if life and history had cheated him; he thought of ending his life by drowning himself in a river, but standing by the river and watching the continuous flow of the water, he reads a message and finds the strength to live.

It was first published in *Penpoint* number 11 in October 1961. It was then reproduced in *Transition* in January 1962. *Transition* was a new magazine, the first issue dated November 1961. Its founder, Rajat Neogy, was born and raised in Kampala. His mother was the deputy headmistress of the Kololo

School; his father, the headmaster of another primary school. Rajat Neogy, his brother Rathin, and his sister Chitra were schooled in Kololo and the Old Kampala Secondary School.[1]

Rajat's entrepreneurial skills began to show at the Old Kampala Secondary where he brought out a nicely produced magazine, cyclostyled and well bound, that he named *Friends*. The name is symbolic of what later animated the news magazine, *Transition*, which he started after returning from further studies in England: its pages were a meeting ground of literary friends. In its literary ambition, content, production, and presentation, the magazine was unlike anything seen in Kampala before, its very title suggesting liminal space between the old and the new. It was one of the signs of the New Uganda.

Neogy became a fixture of the social scene in Kampala. His parties, unlike others around Makerere or among the expatriate set around Kololo, were a literary salon that attracted writers, artists, and singers of all races, heralds of a new, confident Uganda. It was at one such party that I first met Barbara Kimenye. Whether making an entrance, sitting down, or moving around the room, she talked and interacted with guests with the ease of one who was aware of her looks and dress, indeed one who accepted the fact that all eyes, male and female, were fixed on her person and motion.

I was surprised when she came over to where I sat, told me she had read my story in *Transition*, and talked to me as if I were an established writer. It became a habit: every time we met at Rajat's parties, she would find the time to sit by me and talk about writing. It seemed a contradiction. This tall, party-dressed, beautiful lady, private secretary to Kabaka, king of Buganda, from a mysterious background with alluring hints of sojourns in Jamaica, England, Tanganyika, and Uganda had this keen interest in such mundane things as writing, particularly by a student whose claims to fame were a short story in *Transition* and a few others in an English Department magazine.

She did finally mention her own interest in writing. Barbara would turn out to be one of the leading writers in Uganda and Africa, the author of the Moses series and one of the most articulate voices of the new Africa. Behind the party glamour was a very sensitive soul and an incredibly playful imagination.

Transition, a magazine around which budding writers grouped, soon attracted some of the leading African intellectuals within and outside Uganda. At the time of my invitation, however, *Transition* was still in its childhood. Was it possible that my appearances in *Penpoint* had occasioned the letter from Paris, from an organization that called itself the Society for Cultural Freedom? But then, not every contributor to *Penpoint* had been called to the feast. Could those people in Paris have known about the piece in *Transition*? The magazine marked my own literary transition from a student who wrote for a department's venue to a writer in the world. Not that I believed it, the designation of a writer, but I concluded that it was my appearance in *Transition* that made readers outside the walls of Makerere take note of me.

Then I remembered that the letter had come to me through the Makerere Extra-Mural Department. I had once shown Gerald Moore one of the early drafts of the manuscript of what I then called "The Black Messiah." He invited me to his campus house, and on the veranda, he talked a great deal about the new Nigerian writers, the magazine *Black Orpheus*, the Mbari Clubs in Nigeria, and the writers, the guitar-playing Wole Soyinka in particular. Moore talked about them with the familiarity of social friends. When finally he came around to my manuscript, he asked me if some black women had blue eyes. I asked why. Because, he said, I had described one of the women characters in "The Black Messiah" as having beautiful blue eyes. I was so embarrassed that I hardly paid much attention to what else he said about the manuscript. I just wanted to go back to my room and correct this business about blue eyes. I had read too many novels by white writers, and was seeing a black African woman through European eyes.

I assumed that Gerald Moore, the East African point man for the conference organizers, must have put my name forward after reading "The Black Messiah." I was never quite sure, just as I was not sure why Makerere had been chosen as the venue of the first ever continent-wide Conference of African Writers of English Expression, unless with the aim of stimulating writing in East Africa, assumed to be lagging behind West and South Africa.

Whatever prompted the invitation and the venue, it was thrilling when June 1962 came and I found myself among the big names of the time, which included Ezekiel[2] Mphahlele, the main organizer, and Bloke Modisane, Lewis Nkosi, and Arthur Maimane—all South Africans in exile; Wole Soyinka, Chinua Achebe, Christopher Okigbo, J.P. Clark, and Donatus Nwoga, all from Nigeria; Kofi Awoonor (then going under the name Kofi Awoonor-Williams) of Ghana; and our East African contingent of Grace Ogot, Rebecca Njau, and three *Penpoint* writers, Jonathan Kariara, John Nagenda, and me. Rajat Neogy and his *Transition* were very much present: it was as if the magazine and the conference were born of the same moment of East Africa in transition and needed each other. From the Caribbean came Arthur Drayton; and from the United States, Langston Hughes, who had recently published *Ask Your Mama*, and Saunders Redding, then a prominent African American critic.

Langston Hughes gave the gathering breadth of geography and depth of history. He was one of the key figures in the Harlem Renaissance, which had influenced the founders of Négritude. He had been to the Black Writers Congresses in Paris in 1956 and Rome in 1959, both attended by the great names of the black world, among them Frantz Fanon, Aimé Césaire, Sédar Senghor, and Richard Wright. Thus Hughes's presence in Kampala gave the Makerere conference symbolic connections to the Rome and Paris Congresses, both organized by the great literary magazine *Présence Africaine*, founded and edited by Alioune Diop.

I knew less about Hughes's works and connections with history than his celebrity status; the year before, Arna Bontemps, poet and novelist of the Harlem Renaissance, had visited Makerere and talked to us about Langston Hughes, the Harlem Renaissance, and their friendship and collaboration.

The proceedings were held in Northcote, my home turf, so I felt like a host to a pan-Africanist gathering that began June 11 and ended on June 17, 1962.

The conference, hailed as the first get-together of African authors writing in English anywhere in the world, was convened by the Mbari Writers' and Artists' Club of Ibadan, Nigeria, in collaboration with the Department of Extra-Mural Studies of Makerere College, and sponsored by the Congress of Cultural Freedom. There was some self-reinforcement going on here, since the Mbari Club had been set up in 1961 with the help of the Congress of Cultural Freedom.

It was an impressive gathering of twenty-nine writers, five editors of political and literary reviews, four critics, representatives of five publishing houses (British and American, but mostly British), and three observers from French-speaking countries—forty-five participants in all.

The conference was divided into discussion papers, critics' time, with sessions on the state of the novel, the theater, poetry, and the short story in general, plus one session on the short story in East Africa, which meant my work and that of John Nagenda and Jonathan Kariara.

II

The conference had left out writers in African languages, so it was interesting that the opening session was dominated by heated discussions of what constituted African literature, generating a scathing response from one who was not even there. Obi Wali argued, in an article in *Transition* number 10, an issue devoted to a review of the conference, that African literature written in European languages was leading to a dead end.

But for me, a writer in his very beginnings, the most important discussions were not about philosophy and ideology but rather the specifics of texts, elements of the craft of writing.

In the novel session, Achebe's *Things Fall Apart* and Alex La Guma's *A Walk in the Night* occupied center stage as different models of realism. Alex La Guma was then under house arrest and Dennis Brutus was in prison, both for their anti-apartheid activism. Brutus's collection of poetry, *Sirens Knuckles Boots*, and La Guma's *A Walk in the Night* had just been released by the Mbari writers club of Nigeria. Brutus's clarity of images was often compared and contrasted, in his favor, with Christopher Okigbo's *Arcanum*. In person, Okigbo was one of the more accessible writers in the conference. Years later, he would die as a soldier on the side of Biafra in the Nigerian Civil War. At the conference, he was an energetic, charismatic young man who dismissed the critics who said his writing was dense and inaccessible and that he was overinfluenced by Gerald Manley Hopkins, Ezra Pound, and T. S. Eliot with what became a famous quip. He said he wrote his poetry for poets.

And then came the short-fiction session on East Africa. My short story, "The Return," recently published in *Transition*, became the subject of a discussion led by Bloke Modisane, then in the midst of writing his autobiography, *Blame Me on History*. Modisane was unsparing in his assessment of my craftsmanship. He found my hero's reactions to the dramatic events and crisis in his life unsatisfactory. "It lacks emotional motivation; the dialogue is used not to heighten the drama but to explain the events." I listened to the various comments, thrilled that my own creation was on the table and generating polite critical evaluation.

Soyinka dominated the drama session, as much for his already considerable body of work—including the plays *The Swamp Dwellers*, *A Dance of the Forests*, and *The Lion and the Jewel*—as for his criticism of nationalistic euphoria in some of the writings of the time. All our sensibilities had been shaped by our experiences of colonialism, apartheid, and anticolonial nationalism. Despite differences of craft and personal politics, we were also united by a vision of a different future for Africa. Ever the realist, Soyinka had already punched holes in any starry-eyed dream of that future with his play *A Dance of the Forests*, itself the subject of heated discussions at the conference. He had cautioned against tendencies in some Négritude poetry to typify the African past as glorious and conflict-free. Because of the stories preceding him, I expected him to stand up and recite "Telephone Conversation," the poem that Gerald Moore would always talk about, or play the guitar, as Moore had described him doing in his place in Ibadan. He did neither. But I did see him once at the Top Life Nightclub, the most famous nightspot in Kampala at the time, dancing the cha-cha-cha, and even some of the other dancing pairs paused to stare and enjoy his moves.

Kampala nightlife was as much part of the conference as the sober daylight of Northcote Hall. Because the conference took place during the long vacation, it didn't have an immediate impact on the Hill and the student body to compare with that of the American invasion. But some of the writers from abroad did create social havoc in Kampala; they attracted groupies, women—white, black, Asian, married or not—who swooned at their company. Some of the writers left a trail of broken hearts and also a few broken homes.

The conference received good press coverage, in Africa and abroad. Writing in the *Guardian* of August 8, 1962, Lewis Nkosi described the writers as "mostly young, impatient, sardonic, talking endlessly about the problems of creation, and looking, while doing so, as though they were amazed that fate had entrusted them with the task of interpreting a continent to the world." It was Nkosi in the same article who pointed out the ultimate irony, that "what linked the various African peoples on the continent was the nature and depth of colonial experience: . . . colonialism had not only delivered them unto themselves, but had delivered them unto each other, had provided them . . . with a common language and an African consciousness, for out of rejection had come an affirmation."

It would be left to Obi Wali to question the premises, assumptions, and implications of Nkosi's affirmation when, in a scathing attack in *Transition* number 10, he concluded that African literature could be written only in African languages.

III

The person I really wanted to meet was Chinua Achebe. I had met him briefly the year before when he visited Makerere and talked with English students. I may have mentioned "The Fig Tree" to him, but I didn't recall our having had a one-on-one. But now I had a big reason for wanting to talk to him face-to-face, outside the formal seminars and plenary sessions. It had to do with a new work, which would later bear the title *Weep Not, Child*.

As soon as I handed in the manuscript of "The Black Messiah" for the East African novel-writing competition at the end of December 1961, something had happened to me. The story about the contemporary Kenya situation that I had tried and failed to write suddenly started knocking at the door of my imagination furiously. In my diary entry of the third of February 1962, I wrote that I had "been thinking of writing some reminiscences, some of my impressions during the Emergency. I don't know as yet where to begin, but I will."

Four days later, I am recording a mix of euphoria and anxiety, which I capture in the entry of February 7, 1962:

I am in a mood of uneasy expectations. Only last week (on Tuesday/January 30), I sent my collection of short stories to Jonathan Cape. Waiting anxiously for reply. Yet I do fear rejection. Also I am waiting for the outcome of the EA novel-writing competition, "The Black Messiah," completed Oct. last year. Handed it in on 28th Dec. Still, I am fearing the outcome. Yet cannot do much till those results are out. I would like to write another novel. I shall call it "And This Day, Tomorrow." It will depict a suffering yet persevering Kikuyu woman during the Emergency. I shall divide it in 3 sections.

1. The woman [burning of house, village]
2. The daughter [the murder of—to death]
3. The son [the son's return]

On February 19, 1962, I recorded my first receipt of a rejection slip:

Received a letter from Jonathan Cape Ltd. in reply to my short stories which I sent them. Said they, "regret that after careful consideration we have decided not to make you an offer . . . we do not believe the collection would be easily saleable in this country at the present time." It was like an electric needle. Could not read. Never been in a worse situation in my life. Not even 30 cts to buy a stamp. No job for vacation. And Minneh needs support. My studies. Guild work. Which I find so boring. I wish I had never taken it on. *Will not give up. Will strive.* I'll immediately begin a new novel. This will deal with a detainee. He is arrested—had not taken the oath—but at the camp he is corrupted by the admn and a man from the forest. Takes the oath to revenge the detainees. The other detainee dies(?). Our hero talks to another who tells him his wife is dead . . .

These ideas and plots would come and vanish. And this outline remained just that, a plan on paper. As it happened, the first line of what would later become *Weep Not, Child* came unexpectedly.

It came during a talk by the visiting Ghanaian sociologist K.A. Busia, a distinguished scholar and academic but also a politician, leader of the United Party, which opposed Kwame Nkrumah's ruling Convention People's Party. His talk, though, remained focused on what he called the travails of education. My mind drifted from the talk. The word *education* took me back to the day my mother sent me to school.

IV

I am back in my village in Kenya. Outside of the demands for land and freedom, there is nothing that gripped people's minds more than dreams of school. I know I have dealt with this in my novel "The Black Messiah," still unpublished, but that dealt with the beginnings of the Independent Schools Movement, which was before my time. What now comes back are images of the children I went to school with: the games, the laughter, the hunger, the ten-mile walk to school and back.

A distinct sentence steals into my mind: Nyokabi called him. I scribble this on the piece of paper in front of me. But who is the *him*? Her fictional son, of course. Name? Njoroge. The name of the man who taught my brother carpentry was Njoroge. But this is not him; this is a boy, and his mother is offering him a chance to go to school. Nyokabi and her words are suspiciously identical with the words my mother once told me. Nyokabi, my mother, and Njoroge, me?

I wake up to big applause. It's the end of Busia's talk. I don't even remember the conclusion, but I join the applause. There's something personal about my applause: I am really saying thank you from deep inside me. I leave Busia's talk in a daze.

In the next weeks and months, I have companions whom nobody can see. Other characters have appeared. They are rooted in my experience. Oh yes, Njoroge and Nyokabi, are like my birth mother, Wanjikũ, and me. Really? There are a few discernible differences. I came from a polygamous household—four mothers, one father, and several siblings. Njoroge has only two mothers, one father, and three siblings, one of whom is a carpenter, just like the brother I followed, and another ended up in the mountains, a guerilla fighter, just like the same brother. It's as if my real brother, Good Wallace, has given birth to two of himself, each phase of his life becoming a separate fictional existence. Finally, I went through primary and secondary school and then to college; Njoroge does not go to college. The story is not about me, but the images that form have echoes of my own experience.

Why had this story refused to form when I had needed it for the monetary award? Why now with no prize in the horizon? The story may not be about me directly, but it's helping me clarify the nightmare that had been my life in Kenya; it makes me feel at one with the land of my birth.

I am living the inner world of my characters when I get the invitation to the Makerere conference. Another prize offers itself: a chance to show the manuscript to Achebe.

This desire becomes insistent, day and night. I have to finish the first draft, at least. I make a lot of progress, the story unfolding effortlessly, following its own logic, but the inevitable happens. I get stuck. But I have written enough not to feel embarrassed about asking somebody to look at it. It is presumptuous of me, but it never occurs to me that Achebe might simply not want to read it or even not have the time to do so.

I choose a moment after we have discussed his work *Things Fall Apart*, and La Guma's *A Walk in the Night*. I give him the handwritten manuscript, my second. He will read it, he says. I wait.

V

Langston Hughes asked me to take him on a tour of the city. Me, take this icon on a tour of the city I loved? I tried to map out the route.

Where to start? With what I loved. Kampala is the Anglicized form of Akasozi K'empala, the Hill of the Impala, originally the royal hunting ground of the kings of Buganda, a continuous lineage going back to the thirteenth century. The

British were deliberately echoing the seven hills on which Rome was built when they touted Kampala as also built on seven hills, on which monuments to history were erected. The Catholic Saint Mary's Cathedral, known as Rubaga Cathedral, on Lubaga Hill, literally faced the Protestant Saint Paul's Cathedral, on Namirembe Hill. Between them was Mengo Hill, on which lay the palace of Kabaka, king of Buganda. Kasubi Hill housed royal tombs. From atop Kibuli Hill shone minarets of the Muslim mosque. Namirembe, Lubaga, Kasubi, and Mengo tell the colonial history of Uganda. Since the mid-nineteenth century, they have been sites of a bloody power struggle among Islam, Catholicism, and Anglicanism for the domination of the Ugandan soul.

What I feared were the stories of the remnants of that history of blood. Older Kenyan students claimed that once, walking back to Makerere from Mengo at night, they had passed through Old Kampala, the site of fierce battles between the colonial factions Franza and Ingleza, when suddenly, in the dark, they found a band of skeletons barring the way. The students took flight; the bones followed them to the gates of Makerere. There were variations on the story, the scene changing to the Namugongo Shrine to the twenty-two Ugandan martyrs burned to death by order of Kabaka Mwanga II in 1887. This time it was the ghost of Charles Lwanga confronting students. Lwanga had often sided with Mwanga in the name of nationalism. As if to clear its good name, the ghost ran after them trying to convince them that he and the band of the converts to the new religion were not colonial agents but faithful followers of Christ, but the students didn't wait to argue with the ghost.

The encounter between the West and Africa in the court of the *kabaka* had always captured the imagination of Makerere students, to great effect in David Rubadiri's poem "Stanley Meets Mutesa," which ends ominously with Mwanga's father, Mutesa I, welcoming Stanley to his court:

> "*Mtu Mweupe Karibu*"
> *white man you are welcome.*
> *The gate of polished reed closes behind them*
> *And the West is let in.*[3]

I would spare Langston Hughes stories of blood, martyrs, and ghosts. I would show him palaces, cathedrals, mosques, the Baha'i temple, and the other monuments to the modern in the elegant residential areas of Nakasero and Kololo. Mulago Hospital attracted researchers from all over the world. A lot, I thought, to feed the eyes and ears of Langston Hughes.

Not knowing how I was going to accomplish all this with uncertain public transport, we walked down the Hill and turned left on Makerere Hill Road to Wandegeya, where I hoped we would catch a taxi or bus to the city center. Wandegeya, literally next door to the college, was a rundown area with a cacophony of sounds from the multitude of artisans hammering scrap iron and aluminum into different shapes to make household utensils and from human voices of ragged-trousered clients in and out of numerous tiny bars that sold matoke, beer, and waragi, any distilled hard liquor.

And everywhere radios were blaring a melody so captivating that even those of us who didn't know Luganda could still hum it and mumble the words:

Yadde oba onooleeta abo
Abalina ssente ennyingi
Nze ono yekka gwensiimye
Ka ntwale talanta yange

It was "Talanta Yange," a popular song by Elly Wamala, in which a daughter pleads with her father to let her marry the man of her choice. He may be poor, unlike all the rich suitors her father brings to her, but he is the choice of her heart, her destiny.

Even though you will bring forward
Those with lots of money
For me, this is the only one I want
Let me embrace my destiny

This milling crowd, its wails and shouts and ribald laughter, and the voice of Elly Wamala rising above them seemed to fascinate Langston Hughes, and no talk of monuments would dislodge him from there. In his casual wear, he blended into the scene more than I did, with my gray gabardine trousers and black blazer.

He tasted the waragi brew, just a sip, and the matoke, just a taste; otherwise for the one hour that we roamed from shop to shop, one pile of goods to another in the open-air street market, bumping against one drunk and another, he seemed more interested in absorbing the atmosphere of harmony in dissonance that surrounded us, perhaps reminding him of his *Ask Your Mama: 12 Moods for Jazz*.

Strange, I thought, as we walked back for the evening sessions: the slum had similarly fascinated me. I signed my early articles for the student information newspaper as Wandegeya Correspondent, the signature I hoped to use in my write-up on Langston Hughes and the conference.

VI

Toward the end of the conference, Achebe returned my manuscript. He hadn't finished the whole draft of *Weep Not, Child* but he had read enough to see that I had a tendency to pile up on a point already made, like flogging a dead horse. The comments were brief but went right to the heart of the matter. Then he added that he had already shown the manuscript to Van Milne of Heinemann. Milne later asked if I could send the manuscript when I had finished revising it.

In 1966 it would emerge that the CIA, or rather its money, was behind the conference through the Paris-based Congress for Cultural Freedom, though the leading lights of the conference, Esk'ia Mphahlele among them, were not aware of it. This secret manipulation was typical of the Cold War environment in which the conference and the decolonization of Africa took place.

For me and the other participants, it was simply a gathering of writers. At the time, what I most cherished from the conference was the fact that a publisher had expressed interest in the book. I didn't know that Achebe had already accepted the post of editorial adviser for what would later become the Heinemann African Writers series, and *Weep Not, Child* would be the fifth in the series, following two titles by Achebe, *Things Fall Apart* and *No Longer at Ease*,

Peter Abrahams's *Mine Boy*, and Kenneth Kaunda's *Zambia Shall Be Free*.

The letter of acceptance would come to me when I was already immersed in the cultural politics of *The Wound in the Heart*. In my diary earlier in the year, I had written, "*Will not give up. Will strive.*" This spirit would later help me stare down disaster and somehow survive to fight another day. The letter of acceptance would give me even more energy and determination to meet Peter Kĩnyanjui's challenge for a major play to celebrate Uganda's independence.

9

Boxers and Black Hermits

I

On the streets of Nairobi, I once bumped into Moses Wainaina, the blackaphobic library assistant at EAAFRO. I couldn't believe my eyes. He was smiling, or rather the permanent scowl on his face had scaled down to a grin. At first I flattered myself that it was the memory of our work together, making labels for the various scientific journals on agronomy or arranging and rearranging them on the shelves, that had effected this revolution on his face. I didn't have to coax the reason out of him. Lady V. had sent him for a crash course in librarianship; a successful completion would put him in line for promotion to assistant librarian to replace Mrs. Smart O., who had eloped with a lover. That would put him in the direct line of succession, should things change. I knew that Moses was prone to embellishing his stories, particularly those having to do with the sexual adventures of his white superiors, but it was clear that thoughts of impending changes no longer bred in him fear of the unknown. Even then he could not bring himself to utter the Swahili word for freedom, *Uhuru*.

But elsewhere in the country people were talking about

Uhuru. The allegiance of the population in Kenya became split between the Kenya African National Union (KANU), whose slogan was *uhuru sasa* (freedom now), and the Kenya African Democratic Union (KADU), proposing *uhuru bado* (freedom with caution). The *sasa* and *bado* ideological lines were also ethnic, KADU's following coming largely from the pastoral communities and KANU's largely from the cities, with the rural agricultural population divided between the two. This division gave rise to talk of large versus small communities, a split reflected in the politics of the Kenyan students at Makerere. Some Kenyans tried to bridge the two by forming the Kenya Students Discussion Group, led by Bethuel Kurutu.

Tanganyika and Zanzibar seemed the only territories not plagued with such divisions, and this unity was reflected in their activities on the campus. Julius Nyerere set the tone by making Kiswahili the national language, with English simply for official business. His speeches were nearly always in Kiswahili.

Unlike Tanganyika's, Uganda's independence was haunted by the split between Emmanuel Kiwanuka's Democratic Party (DP), largely Catholic, and Apollo Obote's Uganda People's Congress (UPC). The UPC had allied itself with the Baganda king's party, Kabaka Yekka (King Only), to win the general elections. This alliance ruled Uganda with Obote as prime minister and Kabaka as president. But even within the ruling alliance, tensions were brewing along ethnic lines.

When, on the evening of October 10, we celebrated the new birth with good food, the chairman of Northcote Hall, Herman Lupogo, a Tanganyikan, had proposed a toast to Uganda.

Makerere, he said, was a miniature East Africa, a place where men and women of different regions and communities could dwell in peace. However, Apolo Nsibambi, a Ugandan, struck a note of caution. Now that we were no longer "protected," he said, we had no one to blame but ourselves for our mistakes, and this was the measure of our responsibility. Years later, Nsibambi, who married my classmate Rhoda Kayanja, became a prime minister in Yoweri Museveni's government. Did he ever recall his cautionary words uttered in the time of bliss? They were prophetic about postcolonial Africa as a whole.

Looming over the joy of decolonization was the chaos of the Congo—Lumumba's assassination, the death of Dag Hammarskjöld, and the rise of Joseph Mobutu to power. Mobutu's ascent is often depicted as the result not of Belgian colonial history and Cold War geopolitics but rather of interethnic and interregional strife. People seemed to forget the fact that all his life Mobutu had worked for the Belgian Army. A few months before independence, the Belgian authorities he had served so well had promoted him to colonel, a kind of parting gift—or was it an insurance policy? We ignored the significance of Mobutu's taking the name Leopard to echo Leopold.

Ethnic politics began to affect the Africanization of the civil service. The constitutions negotiated with Europe called for a smooth transition from the old to the new. It was in everybody's interests, and the young leaders of the new nations were eager to show that they could maintain standards set by their colonial predecessors. Nobody wanted the chaos of the Congo, right? Nobody wanted disruption, right? Smooth transition meant not disrupting the structures of the old. Old wine in new bottles: that was the motto. After all, old wine was best.

Recommendations to fill various vacancies came from the departing senior ranks, which were almost wholly European. They were retiring or being made to retire, but with nice retirement packages paid for in foreign currency to their banks in England. These retirees had already positioned their loyalists for succession à la Moses Wainaina. How do you keep the old intact yet make it the harbinger of the new?

The governments tried to balance the claims of prior experience and seniority with the claims of ethnic sharing and fairness. Thus Idi Amin, the most senior African officer in the Ugandan Army, became head of the military. He and many others like him were promoted to meet both criteria: smooth transference of power and ethnic balance.

The truth of Marx's observation that the events of history appear twice, first as tragedy and second as farce, was being played out in Uganda: the old nineteenth-century divisions of Ugandans, particularly among the Baganda, among the Franza party (Catholic), the Ingleza party (Protestant), and the Muslim party were now represented in Obote's UPC (Protestant), Kiwanuka's DP (Catholic), and the Idi Amin wing (Islamic).

I didn't overinvolve myself in the emerging student political groupings, largely identified with the various political parties emerging in the territories. The only one whose activities I took part in was the Kenya Students Discussion Group, led by Bethuel Kurutu. This group did not want to align or identify itself with either KANU or KADU but created a forum for Kenyans of all political persuasions.

Bethuel Kurutu, Njuguna wa Kimunya, and Ngũgĩ in front of Makerere
University's Main Building

I felt drawn to matters of culture more than politics. I always felt that political organizations ignored the element of culture or viewed it as a matter of wearing robes made from colobus monkey skins, donning beaded caps, and holding fly whisks and carved ivory walking sticks, and of course surrounded by dancers and acrobats. They hardly saw culture as an expression of the dynamics of economics and politics. It was the unfolding politics in both Uganda and Kenya that gave me the theme of a three-act play, which I wrote under the title *The Black Hermit*.

II

The play takes place in an unnamed country soon after independence. Remi, the most highly educated of his community, works in the city and is in love with a white girl, Jane. He hardly ever goes back to his family in a rural area. But two events have taken place in the country that make his mother and the elders want to intervene and make him come back. With Africanization of bureaucracy in full steam, they want him to vie for office and rank and bring back to the community their fair share of Africanization. More urgently, his brother has died, and they want him to inherit the widow: it's part of the traditional social security. They send him conflicting delegations.

The first is a group of elders. They make their case, and as they depart, they leave behind a magic potion to influence him to make up his mind in their favor. On their heels is a second delegation of a priest armed with a Bible and a cross, again making a case for his return so he can help them compete with other communities for the fruits of independence. As they depart, the priest conveniently leaves behind the Bible in the hope that it will work on him and influence his decision.

Remi has to choose among the conflicting demands of love, duty, community, individual, tradition, and religion. The plot plays out in the consequences of his decision to turn his back on Jane and the city and return to the village, but with the singular aim of crushing negative customs, traditions, and ethnic chauvinism and leading his community into the modernity of the new nation.

III

The excitement in the dramatic society and the general student community at the prospect of a major performance at the Kampala Theater was palpable. The feeling that we were daring to do what had not been done before, in English at least, imbued us with a missionary fervor. Years later in an e-mail to me, Gulzar Kanji née Nensi could still "remember the sheer disbelief in general that a black student at Makerere could be so brilliant as to write and produce such a tremendous play!"[1]

Bahadur Tejani, my classmate and treasurer of the Makerere Students Dramatic Society, reflected on this moment in his memoir, *Laughing in the Face of Terrorism*. He recalled one of the early meetings at which Peter Kĩnyanjui, president of the society, asked, "What about the money?" Tejani, as the treasurer, felt the weight of that question, but he was prompt in his response: "I'll find it. Let's go."

"There was so much certainty in my voice and boundless enthusiasm for the new world, that the conversation changed completely from 'Shall we and can we?' to 'When and how . . . ?" Tejani wrote.

Tejani went on to do graduate work at Cambridge, teach in colleges in India, Africa, and the United States, and write poetry, plays, novels, and memoirs, but *The Black Hermit* moment remained indelibly marked on his memories of Makerere. He rallied the Indian community in Kampala behind the project, explaining to them that this was the first major African play in English and it was being staged for Uganda's independence celebration.

Despite David Cook's invaluable presence during some of the early deliberations, this was a student project. And since it was not bound by the rules of the Interhall English Competition, we could draw participants from all the residences. Among the most loyal and committed were Asian Boxers.

When I first heard the term, I thought it referred to actual boxers. I had never heard of female boxers or crossed paths with any, but now, whenever I saw some women walking toward me, I would eye their hands suspiciously. Soon the mystery was cleared up. The original building of Mary Stuart Hall for women looked like a box. People started referring to the hall as the Box, and the residents as Boxers. The devotion of the Boxers who flocked to the cause could not have been any less than if they had been in an actual boxing ring battling forces arrayed against the project.

Pat Creole-Rees, an English Boxer from Tanganyika, was the costumes designer. Led by Gulzar Nensi, also from Tanganyika, the Asian Boxers made all the costumes. "I remember the making of those costumes on a sewing machine that David Cook managed to secure for me," Gulzar later recalled.

"I do remember ironing and getting the costumes ready for each performance backstage, and making sure that each actor had his/her costumes looking clean and in good shape."

Nensi made history as the first Tanganyikan woman to graduate with a bachelor's degree, and much later she made an even greater mark as an educationist in London schools. Her organizing skills were evident at the time of *The Black Hermit*. Being classmates and members of the reading group, we had a lot to share. She was always polite, the most considerate of persons, but I didn't know that she had another side, a fighting side, to her character.

In my time in the country thus far, despite histories of trade tension between the emergent Baganda middle class and the Indian middle class, I was most impressed by the relations between the Asian and African communities. They may not have run in and out of each other's houses, but compared to the extreme social apartheid in Kenya, theirs was reasonable neighborliness.

Having so much to share, Gulzar and I used to go for walks, discussing literature mainly. "I also remember our occasional walks on the campus talking about fairy stories and the grains of truth hidden in them," she recalled. "I also remember us talking about the taking of human life and whether it could ever be justified."

One Saturday afternoon, Gulzar and I decided to go for a walk outside the walls of Makerere. We were going to visit Karienye Yohanna and his family. The college had not made any provision for married couples. Women who became pregnant had to end their studies, but the men who made them pregnant did not. If married, both could continue with their studies, but they had to find a place to live outside the gates of the college. Karienye lived in Naakulabye, between the Kasubi Royal Tombs and the Makerere Main Gate. Naakulabye was also the location of the Club Suzana, which would soon rival and outlive Top Life in Mengo, but that was not our destination. It was daytime, and it was really nice to have a purposeful walk outside the gates of our ivory tower. Moses Karienye had started writing for newspapers, so he and I had a lot in common as budding student journalists.

We turned right into the road from Wandegeya and walked on the side, engrossed in literary conversation. We had hardly crossed Sir Apollo Kaggwa Road when suddenly cars from opposite sides stopped, some hooting to draw our attention. They were all Indians, and I assumed that they knew her. No, she said and continued. More cars stopped behind the others. Then loudly and aggressively the drivers started offering Gulzar a ride to wherever *she* wanted to go, completely ignoring the fact that we were together. I was scared, because it seemed they were ready to drag her by force into one of the cars or attack me or both of us. It would have been two against a mob. She stood her ground and told them to mind their own business. Eventually they drove off, still hooting aggressively. I offered to break the walk and return to the ivory tower, but she was adamant that we continue. Though she was obviously shaken, her reaction was the very definition of courage and moral outrage. But the confrontation also showed me a side of Uganda I had not encountered before.

The incident made me appreciate even more what *The Black Hermit* production as a whole was doing. It brought into one mission students of different races, communities, and genders.

The cast alone included four Ugandans, two Kenyans, one Malawian, one Tanganyikan, one Asian, and one Briton.[2]

John Agard, a Ugandan of Papua New Guinea origins, played the lead African male. Though a student, Agard was already famous as the goalkeeper of the Uganda soccer team. He had a stage presence matched only by his defiance of gravity in real life as he smoothly reached out for a soccer ball in the sky. Though not dark, his skin was not so extremely light that it would interfere with realism.

But an Asian for the lead African woman? Susie Tharu, née Ooman, had auditioned for the part. As an actress, there was no role she couldn't play and play well. But a black mother?

Mixed or blind casting is different from casting all the actors in a play from one race. At Alliance, all the Shakespeare characters were played by Africans in seventeenth-century English robes. At Makerere we had done *Macbeth* in African robes. In both cases, it was not a mixed cast. But having a white- or brown-skinned person play the role of a black mother?

This was not the first time I was facing the dilemma and challenges of people of one race playing another race in blind casting. The dilemma had earlier confronted me during the last Interhall English Competition, at which I had entered *The Wound in the Heart* for Northcote. We didn't have women in our Hall. Mĩcere Mũgo became one of the first associate or honorary female members later, but at the time even that provision was not there.

In previous years, the rules for the Interhall English Competition forbade any help from other halls. Mary Stuart Hall, the only one for girls, was a rival. Girls played boys. Boys played girls, as in my 1961 entrant, *The Rebels*, for Northcote.

But even when in 1962 the rules were relaxed to allow for minimal borrowing of talent from the other residences, old habits died hard.

These old habits stood in the way of my getting an African Boxer to play Wangari, the black mother, in Northcote's *The Wound in the Heart*. Paula Bernak, one of the second batch of American teachers, came to the rescue. Problem. She was white, with blonde hair, deep blue eyes, and an American accent. We decided to dress her in a long skirt and cover her head with a scarf. This took care of the body. The face was a challenge. We decided to paint her black. But we couldn't blacken the eyelids and lips or do anything about her blue eyes. In dress rehearsal, some of the black paint wore off. She looked like a ghost from a bad minstrel show. It created a very jarring visual impression, undermining the tragic overtones of the play.

For the actual show of the *Wound*, we settled for the long dress and the scarf. No painting Paula's face. Unfortunately we opted for the change at the last moment, and patches of black remained, like camouflage paint that went wrong. Throughout the ordeal, Paula remained a good sport, and after a few lines, the audience forgot all about her accent and accepted the African character she portrayed. Even the patches of black acted as suggestions that she was merely playing a role. We opted out in time. *The Wound in the Heart* won.

This experience was in the back of my mind. I gave Susie the role, but I was clear that I wouldn't mask her face with makeup. I didn't have to.

Susie, born in Kampala, had had an unorthodox multicultural upbringing that enabled her to feel at ease in the role, even when auditioning. Not the least of that unorthodoxy was being home-schooled by her maternal grandfather in English, math, and Malayalam. This enabled the seven-year-old to join the Norman Godinho School, mainly for Goans, at grade four. She then moved to Aga Khan School, mainly for Ismailis, then to Kololo[3] Government Indian School, for Indians, and then to King's College Budo, a secondary school mainly for Africans. She was the only Indian student among blacks, and her father was the only Indian among white teachers. Then she had a nine-month stint working for the *Uganda Argus*, one of her assignments being to cover the new Uganda Parliament, the product of the independence that *The Black Hermit* was meant to celebrate. She entered Makerere in 1962, at nineteen, fresh from the parliament beat. Susie went on to graduate from Oxford and author many books. Years later, we met in Leeds, in London, in Irvine, California, and in Hyderabad in India, where she was a professor at the Central Institute for English and Foreign Languages. Each time, after catching up on the books we had written or news of mutual friends, we would come back to *The Black Hermit* and her role as the black mother.

As it turned out, I didn't have to do anything about her brown skin and long silky hair. A long dress and a scarf on the head was all that was needed to transform her into an African mother. She and John Agard became a perfect match; they made a charismatic duo of mother and son, around which the cast unified.

IV

Readings revealed weaknesses in the text. I tweaked the script constantly. Kathy Sood, the secretary of the production, played a daily role in the continual revisions of the script. She became editor, dramaturge, and keeper of records.

Kathy was the only English Boxer in the department. Actually she was the second of two or three white students in the history of the department,[4] the previous and first being Michael Woolman, son of the bursar of Mitchell Hall, an Australian, in 1957. There had been a few others scattered in other departments. After the American invasion, white students became more visible, but they came for a short period only. Kathy was the exception in our times, and even she did not complete all five years.

She was a year behind me in the honors program. Small in stature with bright blue eyes, she was always very quiet, shy. That's why what she did on one afternoon seemed crazily out of character. We were looking at a section of the script where Remi is addressing his followers; they keep cheering him wildly, calling him "Uncle!" First she asked me, "Why do they call him uncle? He can't be their relative. Is it an honorific title, part of the African extended family system?"

I realized she probably didn't attend the Student Guild assemblies, where the slogan was used freely. Especially when a speaker makes a good point and the audience wants it repeated, they shout, "Uncle! Uncle!" I explained.

Kathy burst out laughing—a belly laugh. She wiped off tears, I wondering what was so funny about a common slogan. She calmed down enough to say, "Encore! Encore! It's French for 'again.'"

Well, it was my turn to laugh. I had always assumed the students were calling out "Uncle!" though I could never figure out why, but I had rationalized it by thinking of the children's game in which the victor forces the fallen to cry uncle. I assumed that the audience had felt overpowered by the speaker!

I crossed out each "Uncle!"

For rehearsals, I drew from my experiences with my two one-act dramas, *The Rebels* in 1961 and *The Wound in the Heart*, in 1962. Mainly, though, I relied on my work as assistant director of *Macbeth* in African robes.

V

I had never gone through a whole production, even for my one-act dramas, without running into a crisis. It's probably in the nature of theater, where so many individuals and egos are working together, learning that theater is the original all-for-one and one-for-all. But in *The Black Hermit* production, I was most surprised by the quarter from which the crisis came, the timing, making it more intensely felt.

Pat Creole-Rees was in charge of costumes and scenery. She had auditioned for the role of Jane, Remi's girlfriend in the city. But in real life she was also dating Agard, who played Remi. Because they were close in real life, I assumed that they would find more easily the extra time for rehearsals on their own. The passion of private life would somehow rub off on the public show. It just didn't work on the stage. She was such a wooden actor that, deep into the rehearsals, it became clear she would never be able to carry it off. And yet passion between them was necessary to explain why Remi is so emotionally wedded to the city as to forget his ties to the village. There may have been a lot of chemistry between them in real

Actors in *The Black Hermit* (Pat Creole-Rees in the top left corner)

life, but there was not the slightest chemistry between them as actors.

I brought in Cecelia Powell, an English student, a would-be teacher who was in Makerere for an orientation program in the Education Department. Taking the role away from Pat brought the production to a standstill. She cried and threatened to withdraw from the production team altogether. John was in a dilemma: he couldn't show too much enthusiasm for Cecelia, and at one time, he threatened to withdraw, which would have killed the production. I put my foot down. It was terrible, but this was a case where for-all had to take precedence over for-one. I suspected that even John could see that Pat couldn't do it; he was halfhearted in his threats to withdraw.

To her credit, once Pat accepted the inevitable, she never let

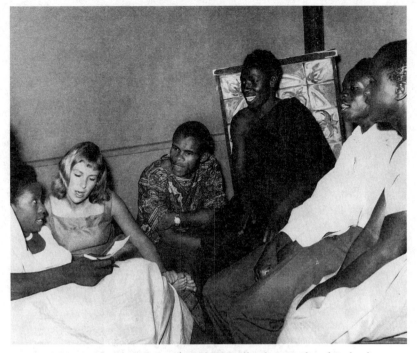

Actors in *The Black Hermit* (Cecelia Powell, John Agard, and Bethuel
Kurutu, in black, are in the middle)

the incident interfere with her work on costumes and scenery.
She devoted all her energies to ensuring that all the other parts
of the project held together. She was a team player through
and through.

One day I went to the city with her to help her identify
material she needed to buy for the play. She went into a store
to check on something, and I waited for her outside. One
of the *kabaka*'s policemen stopped me and demanded that I
show evidence of having paid local government poll taxes. He
clearly mistook me for a Muganda, and my attempt to explain
myself made matters worse. I remembered a similar incident
in Kenya after Alliance High School, which had landed me in
remand prison and then in court. But then Pat came out of the

THE BLACK HERMIT

PLANS to make Africans in Kampala feel that the National Theatre is theirs, are being put into action by the Makerere Dramatic Society, Mr. Ron Reddick its Publicity Secretary, told the *Uganda Argus*.

The Society is presenting a new play—"The Black Hermit", at the theatre from Friday to Sunday.

The play, written by a Kenya Makerere student, James Ngugi, has a topical theme of independence. Said Mr. Reddick:—"We want to put African drama on the map, so that, we can raise the presentation of African drama in the world."

Production of the play is under the direction of a newly-arrived British lecturer at Makerere, Mr. David Cook.

Mr. Reddick said that they are expecting a big audience on all the three days, and some V.I.P.s on Friday—the opening day.

Uganda Argus, November 14, 1962

shop. The policeman saluted and asked her, "Madam, is this your servant?" She said yes, and he let me go.

VI

Stories about the production started appearing in the main newspaper, the *Uganda Argus*, courtesy of the publicity efforts of Ronnie Reddick, one of the new batches of Teachers for East Africa. The story in the November 14, 1962, issue said the

FROM UGA

November 17ᵗʰ 1962; Pag

R. Mazagg. The couple are pictured on right.

" Prize for " 'Hermit' author

A SPOKESMAN of the East African Creative Writing Competition Committee said that the Minister of Community Development, Mr. Kalule-Settala, will present a prize of 500/- to Mr. James Ngũgi, the author of "The Black Hermit" during the performance of the play at the National Theatre, Kampala.

Mr. Ngugi is a student at the University College of East Africa, Makerere. He is a Kikuyu and he is writing about Kikuyu life. Mr. Ngugi is the first African in East Africa to write a play of such a high standard, said a member of the Committee.

★

Uganda Argus, November 17, 1962

Makerere Students' Dramatic Society was putting into action "plans to make Africans in Kampala feel that the National Theater is theirs."

We were not the first to make that attempt. Wycliffe Kiyingi-Kagwe had had successful runs at the theater with his Luganda play, *Gwosussa Emwanyi* (The One You Despise), but these were matinees only, on weekdays, when the theater was not in use for European or English-language drama. Ours was the first to claim a space in prime time at the theater.

The next story upped the drama, for me at least. Since submitting the manuscript of "The Black Messiah" for the novel competition in December 1961, I had not heard a word from the East African Literature Bureau. Then a story in the *Uganda Argus* of November 17, under the headline PRIZE FOR "HERMIT" AUTHOR, broke the news of my novel having won the Novel Writing Competition. It quoted a spokesman of the East African Creative Writing Competition Committee announcing that Mr. Kalule-Settala, minister of community development, would present me with the prize on the night of the play's performance.

It was as if the various literary threads in my life had chosen this moment to come together. The *Uganda Argus* of November 19 ended another story on the forthcoming production of *The Black Hermit* with the breaking news that my second novel, *Weep Not, Child*, had been accepted for publication in the Heinemann African Writers series.

I had already gotten a letter to that effect: William Heinemann would bring out the hardcover and Heinemann Educational, the softcover. I didn't understand the difference between William and Educational or between hard and soft covers: a book was a book, and the imprint thrilled me. Heinemann had published some of the canonical authors I was reading in my honors class: Joseph Conrad, Graham Greene, D.H. Lawrence. Was I going to join the club? Could this be happening to me?

A contract confirmed the fact. It was my first book contract ever, and I readily signed it without fully grasping the implications of any of the clauses. I signed away all rights, which meant the publisher held world rights. The offer alone, cemented by the contract, was a first for a Makerere student.

Black Hermit

MAKERERE College Dramatic Society is rehearsing an original play, "Black Hermit", by James Ngugi, for presentation at the National Theatre on November 16, 17 and 18.

The Society claims to be the first to produce a full-scale play by an East African author. *Black Hermit* is in the three acts, and Mr. Ngugi has tried to probe some of the problems facing an African country after independence.

It deals with a sensitive nationalist leader who goes into seclusion after independence. But he finds he cannot run away. John Agard, well known as a footballer, plays the leading part, while other roles will be played by Rhoda Kayanja, Peter Kinyanjui and Susie Oommen.

Mr. Ngugi has just had his second novel, *Weep Not, Child*, accepted for publication in Heinemann's African Writers Series.

★

Uganda Argus, November 19, 1962

Breaking amid the hurly-burly of rehearsals, the news from London was a shower of blessings and certainly helped publicity. We bought space in the *Uganda Argus*, touting the show as dramatic, tragic, romantic, and adventurous, anything that might stick, and then the formal announcement: The Makerere Students Dramatic Society presents a play about problems

November 15th 1962; Page................

National Theatre
OF UGANDA
P.O. Box 3187   Phone 54567/9

THE MAKERERE COLLEGE DRAMATIC
SOCIETY presents a play about problems
of independence.   Its A MUST for the
citizens of a NEW UGANDA

Romantic, Adventurous

THE
BLACK HERMIT
Dramatic and Tragic

COME AND SEE JOHN AGARD AS THE

BLACK HERMIT

Friday,   16th November   at 6.15 p.m.
Saturday, 17th November   at 9.15 p.m.
Sunday.   18th November at 3 & 9.15 p.m.

PRICES 7/50, 5/- and 3/-

★ Many 3/- Shs. tickets on Sunday at
3 p.m. tickets going fast !

Uganda Argus, November 15, 1962

of independence. It's a *must* for the citizens of a *new Uganda*. VIPs would be there for the world premiere on the night of Friday November 17, 1962.

The phrase "world premiere" was Reddick's invention, and it sounded good.

10

Pages, Stages, Spaces

I

My tummy was tight the whole day: so many emotions con-
flicted in me. The stage once denied to a one-act drama, *The
Wound in the Heart*, would now open to a three-act drama,
The Black Hermit. Will it be triumph or disaster? Two lines
from the Kipling poem we used to recite at Alliance buzzed in
my head: If you can meet with Triumph and Disaster / And
treat those two impostors just the same . . .[1]

The problem was in the uncertainty. I didn't know if I could
ever look upon disaster as an imposter or even how to go about
treating it as such.

A lot rode on the premiere. Earlier, on June 16, 1962, as part
of the Makerere Conference of African Writers, a Kampala-
based amateur group, the African Dramatic Society, with
Erisa Kironde as the director, had put on J.P. Clark's play
Song of a Goat. Along with Wole Soyinka, Clark was one of
the early torchbearers of African theater in English. The writer himself was going to be present, along with other people
of the pen gathered at the conference. The reputation of the
director, a local star, and the playwright, a West African star,

ensured great expectations for the East African premiere of the play.

J.P.'s play, built around themes of fertility, infertility, and ritual sacrifice, is a tragedy along the lines of classical Greek drama, the title itself drawing attention to the conversation between traditional Africa and classical Greece. The Greek word *tragōidia* (tragedy) is a combination of *tragos* (he-goat) and *aeidein* (to sing), and in many African communities as in many ancient societies, the goat was a ceremonial animal, ritually killed to appease ill-tempered gods. The sacrifice of such a scapegoat for Zifa's infertility is one of the most compelling images in the play. Whatever interpretation a director may give to the play, the mood is supposed to be somber, reflective.

The director had a live goat dragged onto the stage on the way to sacrifice. The goat screamed, urinated, pooped beads of shit that rolled downstage, all the time jumping about, trying to get away. Goats have never been the most cooperative of animals. The audience laughed outright. The goat and its rebellious antics stole the show. The disaster left an air of distrust of African English-language theater.

There was also the weight of knowing that we had defied the invisible lines that demarcated what was expected of students as opposed to the rest of society. Consciously and deliberately, we had chosen the big stage in the city instead of confining ourselves to the facilities available on the Hill. By billing it as a celebration of Uganda's independence, we had nationalized the expectations but also fears of a letdown. The fear could be seen in Peter Carpenter, the director of the National Theatre. He was expected to aid the development of Ugandan theater, but he kept us at arm's length. I may have met him once, when

Scene from *The Black Hermit* with John and Susie

he introduced us to the resident stage and technical manager, an Indian; otherwise he never came to see even the dress, technical, or any other rehearsal nor gave us any help. From the stage manager, I understood that memories of the disaster of the *Song of a Goat* premiere may have made him reticent. As if making up for his boss's aloofness, the stage manager put his mind and soul into it. He became an ally, one of us.

Among the faculty, the most active support came from David Cook. He read the script and made suggestions. He was also involved in every stage of the process, never once doubting the students' ability to see it through. When it came to set design, he got us much-needed help from the more experienced John Butler, working with the formidable artistic team of Eli Kyeyune. Dinwiddy was his usual boisterous self, interested, curious, and encouraging without adding to the burden of expectations. I knew I had his support, come disaster or triumph. Otherwise, most of the faculty adopted a wait-and-see attitude.

The turnout for the opening night increased rather than lowered my inner tremors. I had never seen so many tuxedos and bow ties in one place before, not even at the socials and formal dances at the Main Hall. Long before the curtain rose, black, Asian, and white Kampala flocked to the reception area, crowding around the bar and milling outside. These social heavyweights were here to see the play? The sight of fellow students was comforting: I was sure of allies in the audience.

But when the lights in the packed auditorium dimmed and those on the stage came on to reveal an African mother in the compound, working outside her hut, my fears disappeared. My tummy relaxed and then tightened again, but this time in excitement. Even I, who had seen Susie rehearsing many times over, was carried away by her total command of the stage. Gulzar Nensi remembers "Susie's superb acting prowess, the chorus, and the mounting tension in the atmosphere." This set the tone for those who followed and for the entire performance.

At the first intermission, David Cook, Miles Lee, and Peter Carpenter came backstage, almost tripping over one another. Even before they said so, I knew by the thunderous applause that things were going well. The excitement written all over the faces of the trio more than confirmed it. They had come to let me know about the media: Uganda radio, the BBC, and the *Uganda Argus*. The BBC wanted a word with me after the show.

The success of the first act energized the cast for the rest, and when the curtain was finally drawn, I felt that the deafening applause would split the theater asunder. The cast bowed to a standing ovation, left, then came back and bowed to even louder applause. The curtain calls went on for some time, almost like an extra performance.

Hidden from view, I enjoyed the applause while adding mine. Then suddenly I heard calls for me to appear on the stage. I hesitated.

Tejani later recalled my vain attempt to cling to my previous anonymity. "Ngugi was most reluctant to appear on the stage," he wrote about the opening night, "and was forced to come out by popular audience demand because they wanted to see their writer. We gave him a standing ovation." My reluctance was not out of false modesty. I truly felt that the evening belonged to the cast. It was a triumph of talents and commitments from men and women of different races, communities, regions, and religions. It was a collective effort by actors, stage and prop managers, financial supporters, and costume makers. Without all these different parts working together, there would have been no theater. It's collective art; that is its beauty, and I said so. If credit were to go one person, it was Peter Kĩnyanjui, the president of the Makerere Students Drama Society, because he had dreamed up the idea.

The success of the first night set the tone for the rest, ensuring packed houses for all four performances.

The only departure from the routine was Saturday night. It would be a brief ceremony, Peter Carpenter told the audience, after the standing ovation for me abated. He introduced a representative from the East African Literature Bureau, who introduced the minister from the independent government of Uganda. Mr. L. Kalule-Settala presented me with an envelope, an award for "The Black Messiah," my novel in manuscript.

II

The night was filled with ironies: I was still a colonial subject, writing and producing a show about the problems of independence. I had received an award from the hands of a citizen, an African citizen.

But the moment I returned to my room in Northcote, still in a daze, the novelist in me kicked in. I was curious about the award. The results had been so long in coming that I had given up any hope of hearing from the bureau. I thought reading and judging the manuscripts would be a matter of weeks, not months. Sometimes, in my impatience, I had thought the manuscript was lost. But following the completion and acceptance for publication of my second manuscript, *Weep Not, Child*, the intensity of my interest in the fate of "The Black Messiah" had abated considerably.

I opened the envelope. The novel had indeed been the best of those submitted, but the judges, didn't think it good enough for the first prize of a thousand shillings.[2] I was a little disappointed. It was not just the check for five hundred shillings, six dollars at today's rate. I would have understood if they had said that none of the submissions, including mine, had met the literary requirement, but for them to say it was the best, announce the fact to the press, and then deny the winning entry the prize they had advertised in their initial call for submissions—that felt like robbery. But I was consoled by the fact that they had passed it on to a publisher for possible publication.

I didn't let the disappointment over the novel dim the glow of my theatrical debut on the Kampala stage. Nor did I let it diminish what the play had accomplished: a blow to the conception that the East African theater in English couldn't stand on its own on a national stage or that the different races, communities, and regions couldn't come together for a common purpose.

Looking back, the night was a double triumph for me: a playwright born and a novelist-to-be born. The wound in my heart as a playwright had been healed. Little did I know that more wounds awaited me, that theater would later earn me one year at a maximum-security prison and thereafter many years of exile. The journey to the persecution began in Kampala and Makerere, all in the year 1963.

III

In a brief review, "Theatre in East and West Africa," covering the period since 1960, which appeared in *Drama* (Spring 1963) and was later reproduced in the *Makerere Journal*, Peter Carpenter highlighted *The Black Hermit* as the first full-length play known to have been written by an East African.

In another review of the production, headlined on page 1 of the *Makererean* of November 22, 1962, Professor Trevor Whittock of the English Department lauded the play as speaking to a continent and the production as the best thing the Makerere

Dramatic Society had yet done: "Today Africa is in turmoil. Uhuru lops and reshapes the old ways, and the pains of growth are hard. Sects, tribes, policies clamor to be heard, jostle in rivalry fearful that the new birth will cast them out. Things fall apart, and the center has not yet been found."

Otherwise the reception of the play reflected emerging fissures in the critical tradition at Makerere.

Gerald Moore opened his review piece in the March 1963 issue of *Transition* with the question: "Should James Ngugi's *The Black Hermit* have been given a full-scale production at the National Theater?" Then he savaged the play on account of its verse, concluding that none of the issues—claims of nation, ideology, religion, family, sexual love, the tribe, though immediate enough to the East African world—had been properly explored. The play should have been confined to the Hill, where students' efforts belonged—strange for a man who'd had a hand in my invitation to the big conference of African writers held at Makerere. His conclusion about *The Black Hermit* was diametrically opposed to that of Trevor Whittock and Peter Nazareth.

Nazareth's response in the *Transition* of June 1963 pointed out that Moore's question confirmed the relevance and rightfulness of the endeavor to make claims on the national space. Nazareth implicitly recognized the politics of the venue and of the content, which Moore had dismissed. Nazareth's responses were the first salvo in the ideological struggle between the dominant formal tradition and the new desire to free literary texts from formal strangulation. Benefitting from their direct experience of colonialism, the emergent critics began to fight the dominant tendency that took Western norms as fixed standards against which to measure other aspirations. Like their creative counterparts, who realized that the story they had to tell couldn't be told *for* them, emergent African critics realized that the ideas they had to express couldn't be articulated for them even by the most sympathetic person who knew colonialism from the other side.

In particular, Nazareth took issue with Moore's dismissal of the characterization of the priest. While conceding weaknesses, Nazareth countered Moore's claims of lack of depth in the exploration of issues by drawing attention to the play's real-life impact: the conception of the padre led to "a whole series of sermons on Christianity by the chaplain of the St Francis Chapel." However, the sermons about the characterization of the priesthood must have spread beyond the walls of Saint Francis Chapel.

IV

I was in a group of students, most of them ex-Alliance, books in our hands, strolling from the library to the classrooms on the other side of the Main Hall, when I sensed something familiar in the gait of a white man in a gray suit walking toward us.

It was Carey Francis, the principal of my old school.[3] He was on the board of directors of Makerere, but our paths had not crossed here. I was happy, even eager, to meet him, but I didn't think he would make me out in a crowd of mostly his favorites, paragons of behavior, some of them exemplary prefects, often cited as role models. Instinctively ready to give way to my seniors, I looked around. I was all alone. Somehow the others had melted away. Doubts tempered my eagerness. I should just walk past him, not try to remind him who I was.

"James," he called out. I was flattered by the instant recognition.

"Tell me," he asked, without preliminaries, "how did we wrong you at Alliance?" Clueless about what could have caused him so much pain that, four years after I had left the school, it still showed in his tone of voice and cold bearing, I muttered confusedly, "No, no wrong that I know."

"Then why did you say those awful things about us?"

I couldn't remember having said anything negative about my teachers at Alliance. The school was an integral part of my intellectual development.

I recalled, though, that I had published an article in the *Sunday Nation* of January 6, 1963, on Christianity and colonialism under the title "I Say Kenya Missionaries Failed Badly," in which, among other things, I pointed out the symbiotic relationship between the two. I accused missionaries of producing a people who cared more about the poverty of the soul than the poverty of the body. But in writing it, I wasn't thinking about Alliance, its principal, or the other teachers.

"Are you referring to the article?" I asked.

"What article? You have also written about it?"

"It was about missions in general," I said ignoring his question.

"But we are the only missionaries you knew?"

One doesn't have to experience a historical act in person to write about it. "I was talking about imperialism," I said, hoping that this would end the matter.

It was not the discussion I would've liked to have with my former principal, whom I had not met since I left Alliance in 1958. I felt ridiculous standing there, holding books in my hands against my white shirt and gray woolen trousers, refuting implied accusations of betrayal.

The mention of imperialism seemed to rile him. He answered with impatient passion:

Don't become a prisoner of isms, so beloved of the politician. Think of this instead: a company of men, of all races, bound together by the highest ideals of justice and freedom and service. Service above all. A proud member of this company is the priest and the missionary you deride. The missionary has given all—his earthily possessions, himself, his body, mind, and soul—to the service of the least among us. Your politician will demand that the hungry feed him, the thirsty give him water, the homeless build him palaces, the barefoot give him shoes, and the naked cloth him. The more he has, the more he will pad himself, even with the products of the ism he says he is fighting.

His politician made me recall a drawing of an overdressed African gentleman in flashy shoes, an outer jacket over an inner one, a toupee on his head, holding a walking stick, and wearing sunglasses, all under a tropical sun, with the caption "Don't copy this man." It was in the book on hygiene that Francis had written for elementary schools, years back.

Could Francis be seeing "this man" in the nationalists now

leading many countries into independence? Or was his reaction a visceral resentment of triumphant nationalism?

He seized on my hesitancy.

"This mad rush towards Uhuru, James, has brought about a politician who demands service to self instead of self to service."

"No more or less than colonialism has demanded of Africa."

"The settler maybe, but not the missionary and the dedicated government official."

"Can't you see that to us they're part of the oppressive colonial system?"

"But why blame it all on priests? Are you saying that we oppressed you at Alliance?"

"No, no." I felt like screaming. He personalized the missionary enterprise, which prevented him from seeing how it fitted into the larger picture of the ism he derided when espoused by me.

"I wasn't talking about you or any other person at Alliance," I repeated.

"Yes, but the priest, your priest . . .

We parted the way we met: without pleasantries. It was only after he had left that it struck me: Chaplain Payne had probably talked to him about my depiction of Christianity through the character of the priest in *The Black Hermit.*

V

The conversation left me deep in thought about missionaries and colonial ministries. I liked Carey Francis. He could be obstinate, even quick to judge, but there could never be any doubt about his selfless devotion. There was also Reverend Fred Welbourne, different, open-minded, but a Christian missionary all the same. Can one abstract personal good conduct from the system the conduct serves? Or divorce a moral gesture from the context that created the conditions that made that gesture necessary? Is binding the wounds of victims of a system enough to erase one's culpability in that system? Can a moral gesture of an individual wash away the sins of an institution?

Then there were also Payne and Foster, one rather sly and shy, the other boisterous and seemingly open-minded, but both representing a narrow view of the world, again, in different ways. Payne, at least, was too humble to claim a knowledge of the African mind, but Foster had imbibed his worldview from a long line of "experts" on the African who allowed their piety to sanction massacres without letting it lessen their own certainty about their place in heaven at the right hand of God.

I recalled my encounter with a book, *Kenya from Within* by W. McGregor Ross, in which I first read that the hymn "How Sweet the Name of Jesus Sounds" was composed by an English slaver. We used to sing it in Alliance High School chapel, and now Ross was telling me that John Newton composed it on a slave ship? Later I would check this, and yes, it was true; Newton wrote it on his very first voyage to West Africa as the first mate on the slave ship *Brownlow* in 1748 or 1749.

Reviewing the hymn in the light of the context of its inspiration made some of the verses sound like pure mockery:

How sweet the Name of Jesus sounds
In a believer's ear!

It soothes his sorrows, heals his wounds,
  And drives away his fear.

It makes the wounded spirit whole,
  And calms the troubled breast;
'Tis manna to the hungry soul,
  And to the weary, rest.

Dear Name! the Rock on which I build;
  My Shield and Hiding Place, ... [4]

He also composed other Alliance High School favorites, including "Amazing Grace" and "Glorious Things of Thee Are Spoken," as the captain of other slave ships, the *Duke of Argyle* and the *African*, sometime between 1750 and 1754, or in his vicarage, bought and maintained by the profits from his investments in slavery, which earnings continued even long after, decades later, he denounced the trade and joined Yorkshire parliamentarian William Wilberforce in abolition efforts.

The sounds he heard were those of the slaves as they groaned in the belly of the galley; the sorrow, that of the slaves as they moaned; and the wounds, those inflicted on the slaves at his orders. The hungry souls were the slaves he starved. The rock on which he built was the rock to which he chained the slaves. Blake should have written that *hells* (as well as brothels) are built "with bricks of religion." The imagery of fear, sorrow, and suffering is drawn from that of the slaves in the *Brownlow*, but Newton wrote as if it were *he* who were suffering the very wounds he was inflicting on the black bodies he carried for sale. The interest on the wealth from a good sale trumped interest in the health of a good soul. Newton co-opts the suffering of his victims for himself; they become spiritual "wounds" of his disembodied spirit. Abstracting Christianity from the realm of the practical and worldly to that of faith and grace in the realm of glory helped Newton reconcile the two interests. He could sin on earth all his life, but grace abounding awaited him, even if repentance came after a stroke near the end of his life.

Had the missionary similarly abstracted the experience of the colony into the realm of glory, where the conflict between the colonizer and colonized was amicably resolved in allegiance to a common faith? Christianity became the religion of empires the moment emperors realized that they could sin all they wanted all their lives and still have their sins washed away on their deathbeds.

VI

The Kampala Theater was my first lesson in the politics of performance space and the impact of performance on the politics of ideas. In reference to *The Black Hermit*, Whittock had written, "It brings into consciousness the tensions of our continent with humility and compassion." We can substitute "the world" for "the continent." Theater is a dangerous arena.

I could not have known it then, but years later, it would turn out that the struggle for space at the National Theater in Kampala was only a rehearsal for similar struggles in years to come, when *The Trial of Dedan Kimathi*, a joint effort by Mĩcere Gĩthae Mũgo and me, would meet with stiff resistance,[5] with consequences that went beyond the confines of the performance space of the National Theater, into those of prison and exile. That was in 1977 in a Kenya that had replaced the Union Jack with its own flag.

11

Coal, Rubber, Silver, Gold, and New Flags

I

The rise of new flags characterizes my time in Makerere between 1959, the academic year of my admission and 1963–64, the academic year of my graduation. But if I were to frame the same Makerere time in terms of global events it would fall between Kennedy's accession to power in 1961, preceded by the assassination of Patrice Lumumba, and Kennedy's own assassination on November 22, 1963, preceded by that of Ngo Dinh Diem of Vietnam. Driving the global politics of this period was the Cold War between the capitalist West and communist East for the allegiance of the new flags. Vietnam was the poster child of the Cold War.

Not that Vietnam was part of my consciousness the way Korea or China were; one of the LFA generals even adopted General China as his nom de guerre. However, I read Graham Greene's novel *The Quiet American* and found his character Alden Pyle's belief in a third force, neither colonialism nor communism, suspiciously reminiscent of Kennedy's 1957

Senate speech in which he denounced French colonialism in Algeria:

> The most powerful single force in the world today is neither communism nor capitalism; . . . it is man's eternal desire to be free and independent. The great enemy of that tremendous force of freedom is called, for want of a more precise term, imperialism—and today that means Soviet imperialism and, whether we like it or not, and though they are not to be equated, Western imperialism.[1]

The shadow of the Cold War fell on events that had a direct impact on our lives. With CIA help, Lumumba was killed, as unreliable in the Cold War; with CIA help, Diem was killed, an ally no longer useful in the Cold War. But Kennedy?

We reacted to his death as we would to that of a friend or a neighbor. The day after he died, those of us having lunch in the Northcote dining room stood up for two minutes of silence. Words were hard to find, as Dinwiddy wrote in *Newsletter* 12, and it was felt to be better that each member of the community should, together with the others, rest in his own silence and reflect on the pain and the pity of the thing. Kennedy was a brilliant and courageous leader, Dinwiddy added, describing him as "a man of hope, who, with God's Grace made each dauntingly difficult task to which he put his head seem possible to overcome." A memorial service was held in Saint Francis Chapel and mass said in Saint Augustine Chapel. The American ambassador, Olcott Deming, attended on both occasions.

Who killed Kennedy was the most constantly asked question as we mourned his departure. There were reasons for this. Through his Algerian speech, his photographs with a host of African leaders—including Kwame Nkrumah of Ghana, Félix Houphouët-Boigny of the Ivory Coast, and Mwalimu Julius Nyerere of Tanganyika—Kennedy had made America come across as an ally of the new, even though there were signs that the friendship was a case of a West Atlantic power replacing the old East Atlantic powers in the affairs of the Third World.

The fact is, the Kennedy-inspired Teachers for East Africa and the Peace Corps were part of our lives at Makerere. The dramatic Kennedy airlifts that extended educational imagination and opportunities beyond Makerere Hill were still fresh in the minds of us Kenyans.

With Uganda's independence and Tanganyika's earlier, Kenya and Zanzibar were the odd members of the former quartet that had been ruled as British East Africa. The independent two worked hard, even announcing the very popular vision of an East Africa federation first in Nairobi, but later giving it a popular base at a rally at the clock tower in Kampala. The rally featured Nyerere, Obote, and Kenyatta in a joint appearance before a massive crowd. Makerere students flocked to the rally, singing:

Tulimtuma Nyerere
Kwa Uhuru
Kenya Uganda Tanganyika
Sisi twasaidiana[2]

For Nyerere, we would substitute the names Obote and Kenyatta in turn.

The declarations and now the rally increased regional pressure on the British to let Kenya go the way of the other two. The regional push, the mounting nationalist fervor within, and the negotiations going at Lancaster House in London, led to Kenya's gaining internal self-rule in June 1963. It was called Madaraka in Kiswahili. My second son, Kĩmunya, was born a month after, the first in my family to be born in a partly free Kenya.

In West African performances, a small masquarade always precedes the big one. When the small appears in the arena, everybody knows that the big one is on the way.

It was as if Kĩmunya, named after Nyambura's father, had come to tell that Madaraka, internal self-rule, a small masquerade, was paving the way for the big masquerade to come, waving a new flag and singing a new song.

II

The expected appearance of the big masquerade terrified white settlers. Jomo Kenyatta, as the first prime minister of the small masquerade of internal rule, spent time and energy assuring them that nothing would change, that they had nothing to fear from black rule. His would not be a gangster government, a not-too-subtle reference to the "Mau Mau," whom the British had termed thugs and gangsters. The man imprisoned for eight years as the supposed leader of an armed resistance was signaling that his government would not be led by the ideals of the resistance.

Ironically it was in Kampala, not Nairobi, where the terror of white settlers would be expressed. On the eve of the big day for Kenya, some white residents in Kampala held a ritual mourning of loss in the form of a party.

White women came to the party draped in Union Jacks; their men wore *sola topis* (pith helmets). For good measure, the partiers reenacted the glorious days of natives being made to carry messages in a cleft stick. Every offensive racist image was revived in what came to be known as the Tank Hill mourning party.

Uganda had been flying her own flag for some time. The racist nostalgia did not amuse the Obote government, which reacted by expelling fifteen of the party organizers from the country. The Tank Hill party and the expulsions were hotly debated in London. The whites were just having a little fun, explained Duncan Sandys, Queen's secretary of state, but unlike the British, who enjoyed such fun, no harm meant, other people were a little sensitive, and the British government had apologized to Uganda. But don't worry: all the fun-loving crowd had their full retirement benefits in London bank accounts.[3]

The Tank Hill party was like something taken straight out of the pages of Conrad, men living in the outer posts of the empire, completely oblivious to threats of change or even actual changes.

III

In my last year, I concentrated on the work of Joseph Conrad, under David Cook. With his pen, Conrad had traversed the world of European conquest and domination from the far reaches of Asia through the heart of Africa to South America. There were attractions beyond his being a member of the literary pantheon of English literature. English was his third language; his Poland was torn apart by the European powers, Russia and Austria in particular. Did he, maybe, just maybe, see Poland reflected in the European colonial acquisitive ventures in Asia, Africa, and South America?

In his characters—who worked for corporations like Tropical Belt Company in his novel *Victory*, the silver-mining concessions of his fictional South American Castaguana in *Nostromo*, or the ivory trading company in Leopold's Congo in *The Heart of Darkness*—Conrad always made it clear that it was not the egoistic pleasure of conquest or merely the pursuit of fame, nor the suppression of heathen customs in favor of Christian ideals: "To tear treasure out of the bowels of the land was their desire, with no more moral purpose at the back of it than there is in burglars breaking into a safe."[4] In his major works, the struggle for coal, rubber, silver, gold, and other buried treasures dominates the narratives and underlies the racist structures of imperial power. Whatever his characterizations of the native resistance, it's clear he was always much aware that the colonizer and the colonized are a product of the imperial process. "The conquest of the earth, which mostly means the taking it away from those who have a different complexion or slightly flatter noses than ourselves, is not a pretty thing when you look into it too much . . . [5]

Conrad's work was like a bus tour of a world where European royalty and Christian clerics drank wine from the skulls of the slain in Asia, Africa, and Latin America, then went to Church to count their blessings one by one. Colonialism was "just robbery with violence, aggravated murder on a great scale."[6] It was a dying world, but one that still had a strong hold on the living, like those at the Tank Hill party.

The formalistic close reading of texts and the Leavisite moral scheme of "high" versus "low" culture that were prevalent in the Makerere English Department were not adequate to study that aspect of Conrad or to help me fully comprehend the dying world and the one supplanting it. To do so would have meant giving a name to what was really unfolding in Uganda and Kenya, which would have meant *understanding* the subjugated world of which the issues in *The Black Hermit* were a vague reflection.

The play had focused on ethnic divisions as the primary threat to the new nations. Events unfolding in Kenya and Uganda were confirming the thesis. In Kenya it was the white-settler-backed KADU, allegedly representing smaller communities, the Maasai and Kalenjin in particular, against KANU, allegedly representing the big ones, the Luo and the Gĩkũyũ in particular. Other communities scattered their allegiances between the two political parties.

A similar situation was emerging in Uganda, as in other African countries, where a patchwork of different communities, each with a traditional ruler or political boss, was trying to form new nations. Turtles come to mind.

The story goes that Turtle was once the proud owner of a whole skin, but one day he had Eagle fly him to skyland, where everybody admired his wholeness. Eagle was unhappy at the attention accorded his friend. He left for earthland without even alerting his companion about the journey back.

When time was up, turtle had no alternative but to jump back to earth. He landed all right but with his bones scattered. A healer had to put them together but didn't do too perfect a job. Unlike turtle, who still holds his patchwork together with a centripetal pull for survival, using the patchwork to his advantage as house and camouflage, the ethnic centrifugal pull was straining the national skin.

Promoting ethnic divisions as political tactic was not a new discovery; it was a colonial inheritance. Colonial capital needed whole contiguous territories held together by railways and roads, and cities to make the mining of resources easier and more efficient. But colonists didn't want the same communication systems to create a sense of national cohesion.

The economic centripetal and the political centrifugal forces were supervised and kept in perpetual tension by the colonial army and police in a hierarchy that went all the way from the foot soldier to the king, queen, or president, and their role was to protect extraction of wealth from the earth. In Kenya, African political associations across ethnic lines were banned until two years before internal self-rule. But white settlers could form countrywide associations, though they didn't need them, because the state served their interests.

The colonial state thrived on divide-and-rule. And within each ethnic patch, the state created a class whose mind-set was molded by the culture championed by the entire system of education, with its rewards and punishment, praise and censure. Even those who would emerge as champions of a new dispensation would have an outlook rooted in mastery of the colonial language. The ruling language was always the colonial.

Colonialism could not have been expected to nurture and encourage its opposite and survive. The class and ethnic divides could not be overcome by perpetuating the same vision that created, nurtured, and exacerbated them in the first place.

The divisions could have been meaningfully countered only by a bigger vision, certainly one different from the one that had created and nurtured them. Thereby hangs a tale whose implications we could not and did not see at the time.

Each successive government pledged to maintain the inherited standards. Continuity was the name of the game, whose rules were written in closed sessions in London, Paris, or Brussels. But these standards, assumed to be the ideal, had been created and maintained by manipulation of differences of region, development, class, race, and even religion. And we had pledged not to change the foundation on which the standards had been created and maintained. We wanted to have our cake and eat it, too.

The structures on which those standards rested were defended by the army, police, and civil service. Even without conscious malice aforethought, those whose lives had been least disrupted by the struggle were the ones readiest to take over and continue the standards. A verse in one of the popular dances said it well: "The players on the field won the match, but the spectators took home the cup."

Even before the arrival of the small masquerade in June, those who had played it safe by design or default or luck were ready to step in the arena. When the big masquerade arrived on December 13, 1963, the army generals and police chiefs who yesterday were hunting down LFA soldiers in the mountains and rounding up others in the streets now marched as the new national army and police force, pride of the new nation. They hoisted the new flag and sang the new anthem, whose lyrics and melody had been entrusted to Graham Hyslop, one of the cultural pillars of the colonial era. The words are good, but we couldn't even trust a Kenyan to do it or, at the very least, compare the different offerings.

The big cheer of the new nation went to a mountaineer, Kisoi Munyao, who scaled Mount Kenya and planted the green, red, and black flag at the top. His feat thrilled millions: the pride was put into a popular lyric and melody that repeatedly called on Munyao to raise high the flag of three colors that signified blood, land, and blackness:

Munyau haicia bendera
Haicia bendera
Munyau Haicia bendera
Haicia bendera

Nĩ ya marũri matatũ
Haicia bendera
Haicio bendera
Nĩ ya marũri matatũ
Haicia bendera

Mũtune thakame iitũ
Haicia bendera
Na mũirũ gĩkonde gitũ
Haicia bendera

Ngirini nĩ ithaka citũ

Haicia bendera
Ngirini nĩ ithaka citũ
Haicia bendera
Haicia
Haicia
Haicia[7]

The masses sang the same theme or similar themes in all the languages of Kenya. It felt good to hear that song and the national anthem. No longer would I have to ask God to bless our precious king or queen, begging that he or she may long reign over us. At long last, Kenya and Zanzibar, which regained their independence the same month, joined Tanganyika and Uganda to make the entire East African region a colony-free zone.

The Tank Hill mentality reemerged in all the territories, but this time ominously wearing army uniforms. Within days of each other and all within the month of January 1964, there was an uprising in Zanzibar and army mutinies in Tanganyika, Kenya, and Uganda. And in all the countries, the new leadership sought help from Britain to quell the mutinies from sections of the army, the same army that Britain had handed over as a standard to maintain. In the case of Zanzibar, the former colonial master played coy and did not interfere. Why were these soldiers doing this to us? At Makerere, we fumed, siding with Nyerere, Obote, and Kenyatta in their reactions and feeling their humiliation at having to call on the former colonizer to talk down or put down the mutinies.

It was interesting that in Uganda the man who started his military career in the kitchen of the British Army in 1946, who rose through the ranks by ruthlessly collecting the heads of LFA soldiers and their supporters, who was left by the British as the most highly placed African officer in the Ugandan army—this man was one of the main beneficiaries and emerged out of the mutiny as a brigadier and head of the military. We didn't realize then that Idi Amin had his counterpart in Kenya, at least. Daniel arap Moi had been inserted by the colonial state into the political process in 1954, in the heyday of the anti-LFA campaign, and he always seemed to be the main beneficiary of every major political crisis.

An aspect of independence that I found amusing was the way the former colonial powers, Britain, France, and Belgium, were falling over backward proclaiming their friendship with the emergent democracies. They promised aid, partnership, everything under the sun to help Africa catch up to the West. They even professed admiration for Africa's proclaimed neutrality between East and West, as long as they never voted with the East or entered into any economic and military understanding with any but the West. There was nothing they wouldn't do for Africa as long as Africa continued getting aid to buy Western military gear and train soldiers in Western military schools. Friends, we are your friends; we shall help you catch up to us.

A great change of heart, I noted, recalling a gem in Norman Leys's book, *Kenya*: "I, on the contrary, cannot forget what these same men did and permitted to be done when they had things their own way, and I distrust any change of heart that conflicts with people's strongest interests and long cherished and dearest ambitions."[8] The colonial powers that had built their empires on the back of the black body now said they wanted to be taken as trusted partners in empowering the black body.

However, these were mere bumps in the road called freedom. The bumps couldn't take away the fact that I now went to college in an African country that had shed the colonial cloak, that delegations from the administration, the oil companies, and other industries were holding job talks on campus, daily. Heaven's gates were opening for college graduates past and present.

We could also see changes in the composition of the faculty. In 1959, when I entered the college, there were hardly any African or Asian lecturers on the campus. But by the time of the big masquerades, Makerere had had a few, including Bethwell Ogot, Simeon Ominde, David Wasawo, Mwai Kibaki, Senteza Kajubi, and Ali Mazrui. Most of these would later play roles beyond the academy, but their presence at Makerere was a matter of collective pride. It was a sign of the changing times.

With independence, I had another way of framing my college times. I entered Makerere in 1959, a colonial subject, and left in 1964, a citizen of an independent Kenya.

12

Working for the Nation

I

It was as citizen that I took the final exams to fulfill the requirements for a bachelor's degree from London University. I don't know whether it was my way of psyching myself or escaping the pressure, but on the weekend before the exams started, I went off to climb rocks outside Kampala with a rock and mountain club of which I was a member. I had joined the club because of my fear of heights. I wanted to overcome the fear by climbing under expert guidance. The club had helped me explore the different landscapes and rock formations around Kampala and beyond. The experience was very much in tune with my awe and love of nature, which had been my inspiration for many of my stories. But on looking back, it was not a very smart thing to have done. Too much relaxation can put defensive nerves to sleep. But I did manage to regroup and sit through all the exams with a degree of optimism.

What a relief when I handed in my last exam! The journey that began with my peasant mother sending me to school in 1947 had ended. The fact that my novels had yet to be published was my only disappointment. I had hoped that *Weep*

Not, Child, at least, might have come out before I left Mak-erere. I had already sent back edited proofs to London, with an unspoken plea: *Please, please Messrs. Heinemann, I want to leave Makerere a published student!* But it was clear, with the exams over, that the publishers had not heeded my silent prayers. Now to the anxiety of waiting for the publisher to deliver was added that of waiting for exam results from the University of London. Either way, word from London would determine my future. But no matter the outcome, with two novels, one major play, two one-act plays, nine short stories, and over sixty pieces of journalism, I was confident that I had redefined the limits of what it meant to be a student.

I started worrying about jobs. I turned to the *Nation* news-papers: I had been their opinion columnist for two of their three years of existence. They responded promptly. They would take me on as a reporter while also continuing my opin-ion page.

Actually this was not the first time I'd worked for the com-pany in a capacity other than as a weekly contributor to the *Sunday Nation*. The *Daily Nation* had given me temp jobs, for which I was grateful because, apart from better pay, they had freed me from even contemplating a return to the EAAFRO crowd and blackaphobic Moses. Michael Curtis was then edi-tor of the *Nation*. I had met him once or twice; he was kind and considerate and didn't treat me as just a temp.

I had also made friends with the few African journal-ists then working for the Nation Media Group, in the *Taifa Leo* section, George Mbugguss, especially. As a journal-ist reporting and writing for the *Nation* from urban black neighborhoods—Kariakor, Bahati, Pumwani, and Shauri

Moyo[1]—in a regular column called Mbugguss Mitaani, he was the Kenya equivalent of the *Drum* writers of South Africa, the generation of Can Themba, Lewis Nkosi, and Bloke Modisane: the tough, self-assured, ties-worn-loose urbanites reporting on the lumpen-life in black ghettos or the shebeens (unlicensed taverns) where pure alcohol was distilled and served. It's not that I ever saw Mbugguss drinking hard, but it was the image conjured by his reporting from those locations. By the time I started working there, however, he was no longer in the field: he was assistant editor for *Taifa Leo*.

Sans Chique, on Government Road,[2] behind the *Nation* offices, then on Victoria but today on Mboya Street, was our "watering hole," but as a student I couldn't afford more than what the *Taifa Leo* lot, such as John Chui and Hezekiah Wepukhulu, could occasionally treat me to. Chui had good sources among the rising politicians and bureaucrats but was also down-to-earth and knew his way around the city. I had never realized, until I met Wapekhulu, that writing on sports could be so addictive. He loved it, talked about it, was thrilled by it. He tried unsuccessfully to get me to accompany him to the games, but I enjoyed the thrills of the soccer field through his narratives.

A newspaper office looked like a marketplace—noisy typewriters and a constant flow of reporters in and out of the office. Motion, noise, and telephones. When a telephone rang at your desk, you were supposed to answer it. It could be news from a field reporter or a reader. But I was terrified of the telephone, and initially I would wait for another reporter to answer it. Word about my fear of telephones must have reached the news editor, who told me I had to answer them.

I hadn't grown up with telephones. In my youth, there was only one telephone booth serving the whole region, in the main post office in Limuru. Going there to "wait for a telephone call" from Nakuru or elsewhere was itself a sign of privilege: you came from a family that received telephone calls. It involved ceremony, with a gang of one's friends, in their Sunday best, accompanying the "waiting team" to the post office, a few miles away, and sometimes it meant being at the post office the whole day without the expected call. But even this became the subject of stories, the envy of those not privileged to have participated in the boredom.

It took me some time to get used to taking notes from a long-distance caller: a frustrating job, and with bad lines, one could spend hours saying repeatedly, "Hello? Hello?" Even the experienced reporters were not thrilled with telephone dictation, and they often passed the task on to me.

Initially, as a temp, for a big story, I would accompany the more seasoned reporters to learn the ropes, but for the small ones, the news editor would send me alone. I discovered that getting a good story was an art. I was once sent to interview an Indian diplomat who was leaving Kenya. I went to his office, and for the next hour he gave me one platitude after another about the good relations between India and Africa and his own work in helping promote these good relations. I took down everything. The news editor did not use my story. The next day, he sent a senior reporter to the same diplomat, with me tagging along. The same office. The same character. But as soon as we sat down, my experienced colleague noted a pin on the lapel of the diplomat. "Oh, this one . . . The diplomat, startled, told a very detailed story of a journey he had undertaken to a village. This story led to others similarly personal and very concrete, not couched in evasive diplomatic language. My fellow reporter's story was carried as a feature.

On another occasion, on a Sunday afternoon, I was sent to cover a political rally of Doctor Munyua Waiyaki. Waiyaki, a medical doctor, was among the many African intellectuals and nationalists educated in Fort Hare, South Africa, but also the least in stature among the big three of Nairobi district politics, the others being the more dramatic C.M.G. Argwings-Kodhek and the more popular Tom Mboya. I had a soft spot for Waiyaki. Not only did he attend Alliance High School in 1945, years before me, but he was actually the grandson of the legendary Waiyaki. But nearer my heart, his name was the same as one of the characters in my novel "The Black Messiah," later published as *The River Between.* The rally was in one of the African neighborhoods, Shauri Moyo. I took a bus to the place. Instead of standing near the platform or near my competitors from the *East African Standard*, I sat among the adoring crowds, taking down copious notes. I had no shorthand and so had to devise my own personal system of abbreviations, not the most economical or efficient.

As soon as the main draw, Dr. Waiyaki, had finished talking, I left the rally so as to write the story to meet the deadline. I didn't know how, but in the bus on my way back, I felt that I was being watched. When I got off the bus, I felt I was being followed, and it was a relief when I finally left Victoria Street, now Tom Mboya Street, and entered the premises.

I brushed off my unfounded imaginings. Nairobi was crowded, after all. Years later, already known as a writer and

Ngũgĩ with Hilary Ng'weno

academic, I met two people in a bar, and after they had greeted me warmly, one of them smiled. "You are very lucky," he said.

"Why?"

"You used to work for the *Nation*, right?"

"Yes, a long time ago."

"Do you recall a day you attended a Waiyaki rally?"

"Yes."

"We thought you were a government agent, an informer; you were taking down every word the doctor said. So we followed you. We were going to off you. You were saved only by entering the *Nation* offices. It was then we realized you were from the newspapers."

Hilary Ng'weno was the other reporter whom I first met in my last temp days. I think he was also checking out the *Nation*. We were the same age, born in 1938, he in Busia, and I in Limuru. We attended rival high schools, Mang'u in his case and I, Alliance. I was about to graduate from Makerere in English; he had already graduated from Harvard with a degree in nuclear physics. He had seen the big world; I had never left the borders of Kenya and Uganda. I had had a longer association with the *Nation*, but now he was permanent, whereas I was a temp. Bernth Lindfors, one of the first batch of Teachers for East Africa, who now taught in Gusii in Western Kenya, took a picture of Hilary and me outside the Ambassador Hotel. Ng'weno was taller than I, but it was a picture of two young intellectuals at ease with themselves and getting ready for a future in a Kenya about to doff its colonial habit.

II

The future was now here, and I looked forward to working full-time for the *Nation*. It would be like returning to a family. I was a little disappointed not to see Hilary Ng'weno: I assumed that he had gone back to Harvard. After all, what would a nuclear physicist be doing in a newspaper office? But the others were there, and they received me warmly, a reunion of sorts. After a week, I went to the editor's office for something, expecting to see Michael Curtis.

Hilary Ng'weno welcomed me and offered me a seat. He sat back in the chair the way I had once seen Jack Ensoll do. He must have seen the surprise on my face. He explained that he had taken over from Michael Curtis, who was now group managing editor or something. He was cordial without being overfamiliar. It was incredible how editorial authority became him, and so quickly—the first African editor of the *Daily Nation* or any English newspaper in the country. In years to come, he would trail-blaze in journalism and television, including owning and running his own influential journal, the *Weekly Review*, but at that time he was the new editor. I was truly proud of his rise to the top, another sign of the new times.

My lowest moments were working in the law courts. There was so much wretchedness in the corridors of law and justice, and it was always Africans in chains, with white or Indian magistrates sitting in judgment. I had to cover all the courts, and I lived in fear of missing a dramatic case that my competitors from the rival daily had covered. My rivals were suffering similar anxieties, so we made a pact; we alerted each other on the more interesting cases. We also made friends with the court clerks, who would show us files of cases whose hearing we had missed.

Once, in an Indian-against-Indian murder case, I witnessed a most dramatic confrontation between a witness and a defense lawyer, a high-ranking European advocate. At one point, a witness for the state answered the defense lawyer's questions with a series of sarcastic yeses as if to say the questions were not even worth a serious denial. I understood her. In the culture I grew up in, a sarcastic response could be understood as denial. But this was a court of law and the records simply put down her sarcastic yeses as whole sentences. When she realized what her temper had made her do, she broke down.

The magistrate said the court would visit the scene of the alleged crime later in the day. I rushed back to the office happy that my competitors were not in the room at the time. I had scooped them. The following morning, the news editor asked to see me. Spread on his desk were two newspapers, our rival's and ours. Alas, the reporter from the *East African Standard* must have gotten a tip about the afternoon session: it carried a big picture of the entire court at the scene of alleged crime. My story was just words, cold words on paper. The news editor was patient in explaining that a picture spoke more than a thousand words, and mine were not even a thousand.

I was the reporter on duty one Sunday in the old offices of the *Nation* newspapers when a call came from Gatundu, the home of Jomo Kenyatta, the first president of Kenya, asking for coverage of a very important event. The news editor assigned me the task. "What's the event?" I asked. A ceremony: some people have brought donations for the victims of the floods in Kano Plains in Nyanza.

Jomo Kenyatta and his vice president, Jaramogi Oginga Odinga, were standing in the compound surrounded not by the big donors of my imagination but by a crowd of ordinary men and women, who had come all the way from Mūrang'a to contribute whatever they had toward the amelioration of

Ngũgĩ interviewing Kenyatta and Odinga for the *Nation* at Gatundu

suffering of fellow Kenyans in Nyanza. I had never met either of these two legendary leaders of Kenya's anticolonial politics that led to our independence in 1963. My cameraman managed to capture the only picture ever of Jomo Kenyatta, Jaramogi Oginga Odinga, and me together.

III

I began to settle into a rhythm in my new job, but I dwelt in a liminal space between belonging and not belonging, between past and future. A state of impermanence had haunted my life since I first left my father's large family for a single-parent homestead, only to have it demolished, forcing us to move to the new strategic villages. Even with the end of the Emergency, and despite land resettlements going on, it was clear that the villages were here to stay.

With my pay, I helped my younger brother, Njinjū, then working at the Bata shoe factory, acquire some land near Kīnyogori, quite a distance from Kamīrīthū. There I built a three-room house for my mother. She had never come to terms with the new village, and she always loved independence and making things grow. She now had a place in which she could root herself. Her smile of satisfaction was sunshine in my heart. I'll never be able to pay back what she gave me. How can one put a price on a dream? The dream for school and knowledge had been hers before it became mine, and she had given it to me.[3]

Nyambura and I still lived in a rented house in Kamīrīthū. After settling my mother in her new house, I bought a plot in Kamīrīthū. It was a quarter of an acre, but it felt like a ranch. It was a strange sensation, owning a piece of earth. For this whites and blacks in Kenya had fought it out: for this thousands had been tortured, maimed, killed. Do we ever own the land? Only its use, for a time; for in the end, the earth owns us, and we return to it, our common mother. We built a house, not a mansion but a dwelling place, for my family. I could hardly believe this. I enjoyed the special feeling of owning a house without a mortgage and having the use of land on which we could grow a small orchard, plums mostly. Nyambura came from a large landowning family, so the piece of the earth may not have evoked similar emotions in her, but it felt good for us to settle in a place we could call our own. Unlike me, my children will be able to point to a home, a place in which they grew up. I had finally put down roots, in Kamīrīthū, the new village, in the Limuru region.

Nevertheless, the future seemed unclear. I was waiting for something to happen on the academic and literary fronts.

IV

It's hard to capture in words the sensation at seeing an advance copy of my first novel to be published: *Weep Not, Child*. I rushed home to show it to my mother and Nyambura and my immediate brothers and sisters. The kids, Thiong'o and Kĩmunya, were too young to care, but I showed them anyway and made them hold it. My mother wanted to know if that was the best I could have done and was satisfied when I told her I had done my best. I didn't know how the neighbors would take it. The image of a successful graduate was a black gown, a flat cap with tassels, and a rolled something in his hands, not a guy in regular wear holding a book in his hands, claiming authorship. But they received it well, and though they could not read it, they touched it reverently.

My father's family now lived in Gĩtithia, where they had moved in 1962. They were some of the many landless people settled under the new independence dispensation. It was some miles away, but I went there, book in hand, to show it to Wabia particularly. She was my half-sister. She was disadvantaged in every possible way but had remained optimistic about life, dwelling in the world of songs and stories, becoming the collective memory of the community. I grew up with her stories. She was the only one who could conjure them up in daytime.[4] She could not see the daylight; she felt it in her trembling hands. She had molded my world in ways that only I could understand. She had made me want to become a dream weaver.

There was no formal launch, just a date for the release. My very first interview as the first East African novelist was by John de Villiers, a colleague at the *Nation*. He reminded me

Weep Not, Child signing

of the incident with Jack Ensoll at the *Sunday Post* three years earlier when he told me that my future lay between hard covers. Obviously, Ensoll must have talked about his prediction to the journalistic fraternity. Otherwise how would de Villiers have known about what had transpired in the privacy of an editorial office? Yes, I recalled the assessment. I had hated it, for I had needed a job right then more than a hardcover tomorrow, but now I was able to value his uncanny insight.

A Nairobi bookshop run by Marjorie Oludhe Macgoye arranged for me to sign books, and I couldn't believe that people would actually line up to have me sign their copies of *Weep Not, Child*.

V

Soon I received artwork for the paperback edition of *Weep Not, Child*, which meant it would soon follow the hardback. The publishers, Heinemann Educational Books, had commissioned the painting from the Ugandan artist Eli Kyeyune.

Kyeyune, brother of Elvania Zirimu née Namukwaya, was my contemporary. He and I had already worked together on the production of *The Black Hermit*. He was a graduate of the Makerere School of Art, founded by Margaret Trowell in 1937. She was a missionary with a vision of emancipation through art, but the marks of the school's colonial origins plagued it from time to time. The story is told of how the clay for sculpture used to be imported from Europe, Uganda clay being deemed too poor to sustain sculpture. The famous slogan by Elimo Njau, "Copying puts God to sleep," and his advice "Let the children paint," with its emphasis on local materials, were in part a response to that history.

Elimo Njau was the student who once accompanied another product of the Trowell school, Sam Ntiro, to Alliance High School, where, to our shock and disbelief, they talked about a black Jesus.[5] Despite its colonial beginnings, the School of Art had produced legendary painters and artists, among them Gregory Maloba and Francis Nnaggenda, as well as Ntiro and Njau. Glen Dias, who designed the poster for *The Black Hermit*, Pat Creole-Rees, who designed the costumes, and Laban Nyirenda, with whom I discussed art many times, were also graduates of the school.

Despite my association with the school, or because of it, I criticized it for its European bent in my last formal speech at a Northcote Hall dinner. On looking back, I see that my

Poster for *The Black Hermit* by Glen Dias (redrawn from memory)

criticism was too harsh and clearly belied by the products of the school and what it had done for art in East and Central Africa. History does not unfold in a straight line with predictable results. The school could be judged only by what its

First British edition (1964) of *Weep Not, Child*

artists did and not by the history that produced it. The dictum
that people make history, but not under circumstances chosen
by them, applies to art and artists as well. Because Kyeyune
designed the cover of *Weep Not, Child* and later that of *The*

Author photo from *Weep Not, Child*

River Between,[6] he and I were now bound together in books and the world of imagination.

A week after the drama of signing books and sitting for interviews, I heard from London again. I had passed my BA

Honors in English in the Upper Second Division. Bahadur Tejani, one of the animating spirits in the production of *The Black Hermit*, was the only other one in that coveted category that year.

VI

I became a writer, which, to quite a few people, meant an owner of books. Wherever I went, members of the new political class would ask me to give them copies. It took a while for some people to realize that an author doesn't actually own the books that bear his name.

Chemchemi Cultural Centre, founded by Ezekiel (Esk'ia) Mphahlele, was one of the first to invite me to read and talk about the book. This was very gratifying. Chemchemi had become a place where young aspiring writers gathered under his tutelage. Mphahlele also traveled widely to schools to stimulate interest in writing among the youth. I was glad to be part of that effort and also a living example that it was possible.

One day I was invited to Pumwani Secondary School to speak to the Form Four class about writing. Khaki-clad boys behind dilapidated desks packed the room. I could hardly believe my eyes. In their midst, similarly clad in khaki, sharing a desk, sat E. Carey Francis. But for his age and white skin, he could have been one of the boys. I had completely forgotten that he had retired as principal of Alliance High School in 1962, only to become an ordinary teacher in Pumwani.

Way back in the 1920s, he used his free time to work with the children of British poor, in defiance of what was expected of a Cambridge don. He then extended his services to the poor of Africa, first as headmaster of a primary school for ten years before his stint as principal of Alliance for twenty-four years. Now, in 1964, he was back among the lowly in defiance of what was expected of the retired principal of the most outstanding school in the country.

I was really glad to see him, because our last confrontation in Makerere had left a nasty taste in my mouth. Among the hands raised in question time was Carey Francis's. Nothing about missionaries, Christianity, priests, or imperialism. He wanted me to expand on what moved me to write. What tips could I pass on to the intending writer? How did a writer balance the demands of his imagination and those of the political moment? I pondered the questions. The only real loyalty a writer has is to the imagination, the muse. Writers must find the time for her, obey her when she calls, and exert the sinews of their being in her service.

In an entry for November 5 in the diary I had started and then abandoned, I had written down an observation on Virginia Woolf's work habits. "Just learnt that Virginia Woolf would write one passage 15 times. Seems my fault. I am so impatient." Today I have reduced this to a formula that I tell any who ask me for tips: *Write, write, write, and write again; you'll get it right.* Writing is work, is devotion. But in that was it really different from any other calling, even that of a missionary?

Right from his arrival in Kenya, Carey Francis was always aware that he was preparing the leaders of tomorrow, although he may have imagined the future as one of enlightened English empire. In one respect, his vision of molding tomorrow's leaders had been fulfilled. The independence cabinet and administration were packed with graduates of Alliance.

But how many of the new postcolonial elite were going to give themselves fully to the lowly of all the communities the way he had done? Already some of his pupils, ministers and permanent secretaries in the new independent Kenya, were beginning to demand their 5 percent from the people they had sworn to serve. They were nicknamed Messrs. Five Percent. If I wrote another novel, what would I say about these five-percenters vis-à-vis people in the streets?

I answered his questions as well as I could. A writer's quest is truth; his guide, social conscience. But I should have added that reference to Virginia Woolf's work ethic.

13

Notes and Notebooks

I

My future at the *Nation* was all but assured, but in time, for reasons I failed to fathom fully, journalism began to lose its luster. I had pinned my hope on my opinion page, but now I wasn't seeing it the way I used to see it. There was no quid pro quo between investment and return, it seemed. I didn't want to quit, but the question of the five-percenters versus the rest began to bother me.

The question hadn't begun with the latest encounter with Francis. In an article I had published in *The Makererean* of August 24, 1963, under the title "The Writer and the Public," I had talked about the impending changes and then asked a series of rhetorical questions:

What effects have the changes had on the lives of ordinary people, the man who daily rides his bicycle to the factory, the woman who daily trudges to her little *shamba* (garden) to coax it to yield the day's meal? Is there a new awareness, a new consciousness broadening the experiences and expectations of the peasant? Is there a conflict between the peasant's hopes and the plans of his government? I also posed questions about the Makerere graduate, "a man who has been brought up in an educational system wholly colonial, with all its prejudices and intellectual slant in favor of the West."

These questions would not cease. There were others. Who were the prime movers of the military mutinies? How come they took place at the same time in the same month in multiple countries? What were the implications of a continued British military presence in Kenya? Why were there echoes of the Congo in the chaos, and what did they signify?

II

Before my finals, I had filled out applications for postgraduate studies. Memories of Alliance High School affected my choice of schools. I had the chance to go to Cambridge on a scholarship given for outstanding performance at Makerere. Despite my appreciation of Carey Francis's many positive qualities, I still remembered that he once told us he believed that no African student could enter Cambridge on merit, except one, Doctor Wasawo, now Makerere's vice principal. Francis's Anglo-chauvinism was the weakest part of his character, and it blurred his vision at times. Although I didn't take his prejudice as truth, I still never wanted to be admitted anywhere as an academic favor or to be haunted by its shadow.

My mother had taught and expected me to set the very best as my standard. For her there was no limit to the best; there was always room to better one's best. Wherever I went, it would have to be under terms and conditions that let me set the best goal for myself and follow that dream. From all accounts, Leeds University felt the most suitable for me. Other people I admired—Grant Kamenju, Peter Nazareth, and Pio and Elvania Zirimu—were already there. And of course, before them all, there had been Wole Soyinka, one of the writers I had met at the Makerere conference.

So I firmly said no to any suggestions about Cambridge. Before I sat for my finals, I had also filled out some forms for a Commonwealth Scholarship but then forgot all about it. I had thought that my future was in journalism, not further academic pursuits. I was settling into journalism contrary to the advice of Jack Ensoll, but no problem; it was my chosen future, and the *Nation* had given me an opportunity.

Moreover, management continued to express its commitment to me by all sorts of assignments that expressed trust—like being asked to write editorials. I felt flattered whenever I was assigned to write them.

Editorials articulate the position of the paper on an issue. In fact, an editorial can be defined as a view that has the weight of the paper behind it. I quickly realized that it was different from the opinion features I used to write. An editorial has to be sharp, pointed, and carry the right tone. It has to have gravitas. The editorial doesn't carry the author's name, which is the point. The anonymity of the writer of an editorial is what makes it an expression of the paper as a whole.

Sometime in August 1964, the *Nation* management came up with the idea of signed editorials, called commentary. With signed commentaries, the *Nation* newspapers wanted to have the gravitas, though reduced in power, but with the wiggle room to claim that the editorial was a personal opinion in the event of hostile government reaction.

Early in August, the *Daily Nation* carried a story in which the United States alleged that, on August 2 and 4, 1964, North Vietnamese torpedo boats attacked the destroyer USS *Maddox* in the Gulf of Tonkin. I was asked to write a signed commentary on this incident.

The *Daily Nation* August 7, 1964, carried my commentary on the "American bombing raid on North Vietnamese torpedo [boat] bases in retaliation for attack on U.S. destroyer *Maddox*." Quite clearly I had taken the American claims as true. Later it was found that the incidents were fabrications meant to clear the way for war. The subsequent passage by Congress of the Gulf of Tonkin Resolution was the legal path for the formal start of the American war on Vietnam.

I felt bad, and yet I had nobody to blame. Although no doubt I was given the general orientation, I had written the commentary in my own words and signed it James Ngugi. My talks with the late J. Njoroge, almost three years before, came back to haunt me. I could almost hear his sarcastic laughter from the grave: I told you! Working in a newspaper means operating within its broad consensus about the world.

This only reinforced some of the doubts and questions raised in my article "The Writer and the Public," in *The Makererean* of August 24, 1963. Was I then the typical Makerere graduate, whom I had described as "a man who has been brought up in an educational system wholly colonial, with all its prejudices and intellectual slant in favor of the West?"

Being born and educated in a colony inevitably leaves scars. But anticolonial resistance was also part of my heritage. The colonial and the anticolonial values were always at war in my worldview, a conflict visible in my often inadequate grasp of the global character of imperialism and the intricacies of its neocolonial manifestation, an inadequacy reflected in some of the more than eighty pieces of journalism that I had published in newspapers and magazines. In fiction and theater, I felt more grounded than I did in journalism, but even there, not all the pieces were free of scars. Hope lies in learning enough from the scars to reach for the stars.

I was starting to feel a little lost. I felt drained. Something in me was dying daily. The *Nation* had given me a career opportunity, but it would not give me what I sought in life. Just six months into the job, and I was already feeling this? And 1964 was not yet over? Perhaps Jack Ensoll had been right after all: my future lay between hard covers.

One morning I woke up and wrote my letter of resignation, the usual one-month's notice. I didn't offer any reason. I didn't think that anybody would understand, because even for me, nothing was really clear about what was smothering me.

III

Michael Curtis took me to lunch. There were one or two others at the luncheon, and I assumed they were part of the management. But I made a mental note that my editor, Hilary Ng'weno, was not among the hosts.

It was a friendly luncheon, but soon I realized why it had been set up. They wanted to know why I had resigned. They talked about my long association with the *Nation* group; they had plans for me. I must have sounded even more suspicious when I said there was no real reason.

Was I going for higher education somewhere?

Well, I had applied but I hadn't had any responses offering a place or a scholarship.

Had it anything to do with Hilary Ng'weno? Had we fallen

out or something? They asked while assuring me that I could talk to them in full confidence. But I had nothing against Hilary. I thought he did a fantastic job. And we had not fallen out.

The luncheon came to an end with thanks from me and their assurance that if ever . . . Well, it was just that.

Collage by Barbara Caldwell of articles about and by Ngũgĩ in the *Makererean* and *Transition*

I didn't think I was going to change my mind, but you never can tell.

Later when an admission to Leeds University came, followed by an offer of a scholarship, my workmates insinuated that I knew it was coming and hence my resignation.

I didn't try to explain. I was just struck by the irony: the British Council, which once smashed my dreams with an alleged hand in denying my play, *The Wound in the Heart*, a space at the Kampala National Theater because "British officers could not do such a thing," now had a big hand in enabling me to pursue my dreams in Leeds, in Yorkshire, the land of Emily Brontë of *Wuthering Heights*. And thanks to the British Council Scholarship, Leeds would alter the course of my life as a writer, academic, and thinker.

I now had yet another way of framing my college times. I entered Makerere in the 1959 academic year, a colonial subject, and left in 1964, a citizen of an independent Kenya. In those few years a writer was born. I had a novel out, *Weep Not, Child*; a second, *The River Between*, in the pipeline; a three-act play, *The Black Hermit*; two one-act plays; and over sixty pieces of journalism in newspapers and magazines.

Even then I found it difficult to use the word *writer* to refer to myself. In my mind, all this was a kind of preparation for the writer-to-be. So on many forms and documents, for occupation, I would put *student*. It was as if I had not yet written the novel I wanted to write. But the desire to weave dreams remained aflame, an integral part of my life.

14

A Hell of a Paradise

I

"We did not know we lived in Paradise," Hugh Dinwiddy would later quote Sam Lunyiigo, a former head of the History Department, who made the remark at a conference years after.[1]

This paradise could only refer to the Makerere of the 1950s and early 1960s. It was not just its location on a hill that faced other hills with poetic-sounding names like Rubaga and Namirembe, on which stood cathedrals or the Lubiri Palace or the Kasubi Royal Tombs.

We partook of paradise in the social evenings in the halls of residence and the dances on the floor of the Main Hall, supplemented by the nightlife in Kampala in and around Top Life, Suzana, and other clubs with live music from resident bands. Music also permeated the dinner parties at people's houses in Kololo or, for me, the literary salons around Rajat Neogy and *Transition*. I realize now that, as a budding writer, playwright, and columnist, I may have accessed social spaces not shared by fellow undergraduates, but in the main, Makerere was a place where different races, communities, and even religions seemed able to work together. It was a place where we felt we could challenge the best that any university in the world—Cambridge, Oxford, Harvard, you name it—had to offer. It was an institution where not to be admitted left a hole that couldn't quite be healed by achievements elsewhere. It was a place where the impossible seemed possible. Makerere was then a place of dreams.

Only in that Makerere did it seem possible that "the wolf also shall dwell with the lamb, and the leopard shall lie down with the kid; and the calf and the young lion and the fatling together; and a little child shall lead them. . . . They shall not hurt nor destroy in all my holy mountain: for the earth shall be full of the knowledge of the Lord, as the waters cover the sea."[2]

But they did hurt and destroy, in the form of Idi Amin, who overthrew the Obote regime in 1971 and scattered Makerereans and Ugandans to the four corners of the world: artists, writers, politicians—no social sector was spared. To Amin and his soldiers, Makerere was the site of an educated elite to be humiliated and made to serve the soldiers, the women among them to be abducted and/or raped. But the new overlords also envied Makerere; Idi Amin, now chancellor, extorted several honorary doctorates from the university. Some professors and students were killed; others fled into exile.

We should have seen it coming, the smoke from the fire of hell, at least. The colonialists had lit the fire. They had exiled kings when it suited them, but they also subtly allied themselves with kings against the nationalists' demands for independence and later against Obote's deceptive "move to the left," a cover for endemic state corruption and tyranny that had little to do with his stated socialist ideals. The colonialists had stoked the tension between Buganda and Bunyoro over the Lost Counties (Bunyoro land taken by Buganda when that kingdom allied itself with the early British colonists), then left it to the new men of power to solve the issue. Above all, they had promoted Idi Amin for his zeal in harvesting the skulls of LFA soldiers, the so called Mau Mau, in Kenya. Obote had accepted the gift from the colony and used it to storm Kabaka's palace (not that the *kabaka* himself was innocent of military intrigues against the central government); his ruthless victory gave him military supremacy. He hoped to use the gift to consolidate his moves to the left, only to discover that the gift was a poisoned chalice.

The West embraced their creation with glee. It gave Amin state visits from Golda Meir of Israel, Georges Pompidou of France, and Queen Elizabeth of England. Only when they saw him begin to behave oddly, not always following decorum, did Western leaders denounce him as a dictator and an example of black misrule rather than foreign manipulation. Suddenly they discovered that he did actually refrigerate the decapitated heads of his captives and feed their bodies to crocodiles. But this was not his first decapitation program, for he had acquired the habit of head-hunting as a member of the King's African Rifles, fighting "Mau Mau," and he must have been surprised by the fickleness of those who now denounced him for doing things for which they had once given him medals.

There was always hell in paradise, the fire at least, only we didn't see it, or even the smoke, and that's why it shocked. For me it was the sheer helplessness of seeing my friends scattered all over the world and not being there to lend a helping hand or even say a soothing word. One's loss may very well be another's gain. Kenyan schools profited from the hundreds of Ugandan exiles who became dedicated teachers in Kenya. Britain, Canada, and the United States gained from the entrepreneurial skills of the many Ugandan-Asian exiles who reached their shores.

I had known Peter Nazareth from our Makerere days to our time in Leeds, and we had become close. His wife was Mary and we played with their names as the Mary and Peter of biblical Nazareth. His Makerere stories and plays had exuded love for the Uganda he grew up in. Now he was "Ugandan Asian." Bahadur Tejani, too: we were five years in the same classes, in the same study group. We shared the same friends, like Bethuel Kurutu, but now he, too, was "Ugandan Asian," exiled from the land he loved. Theirs was the story of Africa.

This heartache would be best captured in a poem, "Snapshots," by Susan Kiguli. Kiguli opens the poem by making it clear that she never actually saw the Indians leave. But she feels their exodus in the story of the massacres in Uganda and elsewhere on the continent.

I see the Indians on a journey
Away from their home
In the abandoned houses
Of our districts.

Every day I think of dictators

I see the Ugandan Indians leave.[3]

Susan Kiguli writes in Luganda and English, and she chairs the Literature Department where Nazareth, Tejani, and I were once students. She dedicates "Snapshots" to Peter Nazareth. Somehow, Makerere survived, but as a shadow of its past. Now, however, with the minds and dedication of Susan Kiguli's generation, it has all the signs of a phoenix rising from the ashes of terror to be once again the beacon on the Hill, seen from every corner of the continent and the world. The Idi Amin chaos will then be just a temporary setback on the march of history.

Of course, Obote had done his bit to bring about the chaos. After all, it was he, the Makerere man, who had imprisoned Rajat Neogy, the literary man, and forced him into exile long before Idi Amin, the military man, executed the Asian exodus. Idi Amin then unleashed the full force of hell on other intellectuals I had worked with and knew: Pio Zirimu, Wycliffe Kingi, and other Ugandan artists and performers. The road to political hell begins with intolerance of ideas and difference.

I once met Barbara Kimenye in Nairobi. She was working for the *Nation*, and her column was followed by thousands, but to me, who always associated her with Kampala, she looked like a misfit in the streets of Nairobi. In my eyes, she still belonged to the Kampala built on many hills, certainly more than the seven on which Rome was built, dreaming up her fictional Moses character and fictional school. The Kampala of literary salons and clashing ideas was a thing of the past.

Yes, we lived in paradise, but it was paradise built on the uneven colonial structures we had sworn to maintain. Was it

The Duke of Edinburgh stands beside Jomo Kenyatta as Kenya regains
its "independence" in 1963

that different from the rest of the continent? By the time Idi
Amin's eight years of terror were over, a civilian Amin had
already assumed the throne in my beloved Kenya. His name
was Daniel arap Moi. He made children sing his praises for
getting them yellow corn from America in times of hunger
he had created. He orchestrated marches all over the country
with the slogan *Karamu chini*, Down with the pen. It was the
turn of Kenyan intellectuals to flee. The dictatorship forced
me to join Peter Nazareth and Bahadur Tejani and many others in exile, where we talked about the Makerere that once
promised us paradise. That, prison and exile, is another story.
But the Makerere where I discovered my calling as a weaver of
dreams will always be part of it.

Acknowledgments

The first public reading of selections from this memoir was at Professor Gaby Schwab's annual new year festival at her house in University Hills at the University of California, Irvine. Thanks Gaby, family, and friends!

My heartfelt thanks also to: Barbara Caldwell for library research, her design of the pictures and illustrations, and her custody of the various documents for this memoir; Doctor Susan Kiguli and Charles Ssekitoleko for archival research in Makerere; Mary Musoke for enabling; Peter Nazareth and John Nazareth for sharing memories and stories of the past; Carol Sicherman for her work on Makerere, sharing information and pictures, and for reading and suggesting changes in the manuscript; Bahadur Tejani for oral and written testimonies; Glen Dias, who shared memories and redrew *The Black Hermit* poster from memory; Bethuel Kiplagat, who reminded me that we lived in adjoining rooms; Dan Kahyana, Kathy Sood, Gulzar Kanji, Susie (Ooman) Tharu, Mĩcere Mũgo, Nat Frothingham, and Bernth Lindfors, who all provided useful pictures, and Lindfors for helping unlock memories with his work on my early journalism; Heather Pesani for unearthing the Makerere conference report; Jones Kyazze, who refreshed memories of the Makerere that was by unearthing and translating for me Elly Wamala's song "Talanta Yange"; Njeeri wa Ngũgĩ, always my first literary critic, who made useful comments on the sections I tried on her; Kĩmunya Ngũgĩ for pictures; Mũkoma wa Ngũgĩ for reading the manuscript and making useful suggestions; Gary Stimeling for copyediting the manuscript; and Gloria Loomis and Henry Chakava for reading the earlier draft and making useful suggestions. Finally, I want to thank Ms. Shirley Ono of Delta Airlines who rescued the computer containing this manuscript from the plane where I had left it during my flight from Salt Lake City to Orange County.

Notes

1: The Wound in the Heart

1. The Theater of Dionysus in Athens saw plays by Aeschylus, Euripides, Sophocles, Aristophanes, and many others. A metal tripod for cooking over a fire was the trophy for the winner.

2. Nazareth is now the well-known novelist of *In a Brown Mantle* and *The General Is Up*. He is also a top professor at Iowa University, an advisor to its International Writing Program, and the editor of numerous scholarly and creative works. Along the way, he has gained notoriety for his innovative interpretation of Elvis Presley as a multiracial, multicultural Third Worlder.

3. *Northcote Hall Newsletter*, 1962, no. 4, p. 1.

4. All her life, up to her death in 2011, MacPherson edited and maintained the *Old Makerere Newsletter*, trying to track the movement and activities of all Makererean faculty members and students wherever in the world they had been spotted.

5. Margaret MacPherson, *They Built for the Future: A Chronicle of Makerere University College, 1922–1962* (Cambridge, UK: Cambridge University Press, 1964).

6. *Northcote Hall Newsletter*, 1962, no. 4, p. 2. Glennie Dias, Ronnie Reddick, Bethuel Kurutu, Herman Lupogo, Emmanuel Kiwanuka, Nazareno Ngulukulu, and Paula Bernak took part in the play.

2: A Wounded Land

1. From research notes of Professor Peter Lehman, which he shared with me.

2. Karen Blixen, aka Isak Dinesen, *Out of Africa* (London: Penguin, 1954), 243.

3. J.-G. L., review of John C. Carothers, *The African Mind in Health and Disease* (Geneva: World Health Organization, 1953), in *Revue Internationale de la Croix-Rouge et Bulletin international des Sociétés de la Croix-Rouge* (International

Review of the Red Cross) 37, no. 443 (November 1955): 758–60, doi:10.1017/S0035336100138304.

4. John C. Carothers, *The Psychology of Mau Mau* (Nairobi: Government Printer, 1954).

5. Samuel A. Cartwright, "Report on the Diseases and Physical Peculiarities of the Negro Race," *De Bow's Review*, vol. 11, New Orleans, 1851.

6. Frank Derek Corfield, *The Origins and Growth of Mau Mau: An Historical Survey* (London: Her Majesty's Stationery Office, 1960), presented to Parliament by the secretary of state for the colonies by command of her majesty, May 1960.

7. Hola Camp, Kenya, Report, UK Parliament, House of Commons Debate, July 27, 1959, *Hansard* (edited parliamentary debate transcriptions), vol. 610, columns 181–262, at 181, http://hansard.millbanksystems.com/commons/1959/jul/27/hola-camp-kenya-report (accessed July 9, 2015).

8. Cited and quoted in *The Guardian*, April 18, 2012.

9. See the story of Good Wallace in my *Dreams in a Time of War: A Childhood Memoir* (New York: Anchor, 2011) and *In the House of the Interpreter: A Memoir* (New York: Anchor, 2015).

10. William Shakespeare, *Macbeth*, ed. Thomas Marc Parrott (New York: American Book Co., 1904), Act 2, Scene 2, lines 83–84, available at Shakespeare Online, www.shakespeare-online.com/plays/macbeth_2_2.html.

3: Reds and Blacks

1. See my *Dreams in a Time of War: A Childhood Memoir* (New York: Anchor, 2011) and *In the House of the Interpreter: A Memoir* (New York: Anchor, 2015).

2. Winston Churchill, *My African Journey* (Toronto: William Briggs, 1909), ch. 5, pp. 88–89, https://archive.org/details/myafricanjourney00churuoft.

3. Ibid., ch. 10, p. 197.

4. Politicians tried and imprisoned with Kenyatta: Paul Ngei, Bildad Kaggia, Kũng'ũ Karumba, Fred Kubai. The fifth was Achieng Oneko, held elsewhere.

5. Aristotle, *Metaphysics*, tr. W.D. Ross, book 2, part 1, http://classics.mit.edu/Aristotle/metaphysics.2.ii.html.

6. Bernard de Bunsen, *Adventures in Education* (Kendal, UK: Titus Wilson, 1995), 68.

7. Today there are many more halls, and Northcote has been renamed Nakulabye.

8. Mitchell also governed Fiji and Kenya, in that order, in the latter place being replaced by Evelyn Baring, who declared a state of emergency in 1952.

9. Quoted in Hugh Dinwiddy, "Makerere and Development in East Africa in the Colonial Period," paper presented at the Conference on Uganda at the Univer-

sity of Copenhagen, September 25–29, 1985.

10. Peter Nazareth, leader of the conquerors, told me details of the story. See also Hugh Dinwiddy in *Tributes to Fred Welbourne*.

11. The other actors included Bethuel Kurutu and Ben Kipkorir.

12. Peter Nazareth tells me that years later he found the play among my books in the University of Iowa Library in Iowa City in 1973, under the title *The Wound in the Knee*. He told the librarian the play was called *The Wound in the Heart*. "Oh," he said. "The book was received just after the Wounded Knee uprising and must have affected the person listing it."

13. E-mail to me dated Thursday, August 28, 2012.

4: Benzes, Sneakers, Frisbees, and Flags

1. John F. Kennedy, Inaugural Address, January 20, 1961, www.jfklibrary.org/Asset-Viewer/BqXIEM9F4024ntFl7SVAjA.aspx.

2. Tom Mboya, who became a minister in Kenyatta's independence government, was assassinated on Government Road (now Moi Avenue) in Nairobi on July 5, 1969.

3. Judith Lindfors, ed., *The TEA Experience* (2002).

4. Bernard de Bunsen, *Adventures in Education* (Kendal, UK: Titus Wilson, 1995), 114.

5. Frank Derek Corfield, *The Origins and Growth of Mau Mau: An Historical Survey* (London: Her Majesty's Stationery Office, 1960), presented to Parliament by the secretary of state for the colonies by command of her majesty, May 1960.

6. See my previous memoirs, *Dream in a Time of War* and *In the House of the Interpreter*.

7. F.D. Corfield, *The Origins and Growth of Mau Mau* (1960) ch. 2, 7

8. John C. Carothers, *The Psychology of Mau Mau* (Nairobi: Government Printer, 1954).

9. Corfield, *Mau Mau*, p. 8, n. 1.

10. Ibid., ch. 2, 9.

11. Ian Henderson, *The Hunt for Kimathi* (London: Hamish Hamilton, 1958).

12. Ibid., ch. 2, p. 22.

13. Norman Maclean Leys, *Kenya*, 4th ed. (London: Frank Cass, 1973), introduction by George Shepperson, 6.

14. Elspeth Huxley, *White Man's Country: Lord Delamere and the Making of Kenya* (New York: Praeger, 1967).

15. Leys, *Kenya*, 9.

16. Ibid., 334.

17. B. Gakonyo, *Comment on Corfield* (Kampala: Makerere Kikuyu Embu and Meru Students Association, 1960).

18. These include Rubadiri, Malawi, 1953–54; Ahmed Abdalla, Kenya, 1958–59; Simeon G.M. Gor, Kenya, 1959–60; Francis Lucas Nyalali, Tanzania, 1960–61; D.G. Ombati, Kenya, 1961–62; Matthew Rukikaire, Uganda, 1962–63; and E.M. Mugenzi, Uganda, 1963–64.

19. Carol Sicherman, *Becoming an African University, Makerere 1922–2000* (Trenton, NJ: Africa World Press, 2005), 334.

20. Patrice Lumumba, Speech at Léopoldville, 1958, Main Currents in African History, course synopsis, Dr. Gregory Mann, Columbia University, www.columbia.edu/itc/history/mann/w3005, under Web Resources. (accessed August 13, 2015).

21. William Wordsworth, "The French Revolution as It Appeared to Enthusiasts at Its Commencement," lines 4–5, www.poetryfoundation.org/poem/174787.

6: Writing for the Money of It

1. See my *Dreams in a Time of War: A Childhood Memoir* (New York: Anchor, 2011) and *In the House of the Interpreter: A Memoir* (New York, Anchor: 2015).

2. See *Dreams in a Time of War.*

3. Ibid.

4. *Mbura ura*
   Ngũthiĩnjĩre
   Gategwa na kangĩ
   Karĩ mbugi
   Ng'iri! Ng'iri! Ng'iri!

7: Black Dolls and Black Masks

1. Kenya African Union (1942–1952). The 1960 KANU for Kenya African National Union was a conscious echo of the banned first.

2. *Tũtirũragia gũthamio*
   Kana gũtwarwo njera
   Kana gũtwarwo icigĩrĩra
   Amu tũtigatiga gũtetera wĩyathi
   Kenya nĩ bũrũri wa andũ airũ

3. See my *Dreams in a Time of War: A Childhood Memoir* (New York: Anchor, 2011).

4. See my *In the House of the Interpreter: A Memoir* (New York: Anchor, 2015).

5. Not her real name.

6. Not her real name.

7. Not his real name.

8. *The Rebels* was first broadcast by UBS on April 6, 1962, at 10:00 p.m.

9. Gerald Moore and Ulli Beier, eds., *The Penguin Book of Modern African Poetry*, 4th ed. (New York: Penguin, 1999).

10. Ibid., 316.

11. Léopold Sédar Senghor, "Black Woman," http://allpoetry.com/poem/8594 637-Black-Woman-by-Leopold-Sedhar-Senghor.

12. Modernist Africana Poetry of the Americas, course synopsis, Prof. Brenda Marie Osbey, Brown University, Two Poems by Léon Damas, http://osbey.tripod.com/mapa/damas.html.

13. *Taifa* means "nation" in Kiswahili.

8: Transition and That Letter from Paris

1. I am indebted to Peter Nazareth for this biographical information. Peter and Rajat went to the same schools, Rajat two years ahead.

2. Later he would change it to Eski'a.

3. David Rubadiri, "Stanley Meets Mutesa," http://allpoetry.com/poem/10502 019-Stanley-Meets-Mutesa-by-David-Rubadiri.

9: Boxers and Black Hermits

1. Gulzar Kanji to me, August 28, 2012.

2. These were John Agard, Rhoda Kayanja, Frieda Kase, Lydia Lubwama, Peter Kĩnyanjui, Bethuel Kurutu, Goody Godo, John Moyo, Cecelia Powell, and Susie Ooman.

3. Among her schoolmates were Bahadur Tejani, Chitra Neogy (sister to Rajat Neogy of *Transition* magazine), and the charismatic playwright and actress Elvania Zirimu née Namukwaya, whose support and generosity and long hours spent talking about many things Susie remembers.

4. Generally there were very few white European students in the Makerere of the time. Peter Nazareth reminds me that there was a Mr. Brian Austin-Ward doing a general degree but with English as his three subjects.

10: Pages, Stages, Spaces

1. Rudyard Kipling, "If—," www.poetryfoundation.org/poem/175772.

2. Worth twelve dollars today.

3. See my *In the House of the Interpreter: A Memoir* (New York, Anchor, 2015).

4. John Newton, lyrics (1779), and Alexander Reinagle, music (1836), "How Sweet the Name of Jesus Sounds," http://cyberhymnal.org/htm/h/s/hsweetnj .htm.

5. See Ngũgĩ wa Thiong'o, *Detained: A Writer's Prison Diary* (1981; Nairobi: East African Educational Publishers, 2006) and Ngũgĩ wa Thiong'o, *Penpoints, Gunpoints, and Dreams: Towards a Critical Theory of the Arts and the State in Africa* (1998; Oxford: Clarendon Press, 2003).

11: Coal, Rubber, Silver, Gold, and New Flags

1. John F. Kennedy, "Remarks of Senator John F. Kennedy at Syracuse University in Syracuse, New York, June 3, 1957," www.jfklibrary.org/Research/Research -Aids/JFK-Speeches/Syracuse-University_19570603.aspx.

2. *We sent Nyerere*
   On a mission for Freedom
   Kenya Uganda Tanganyika
   We help one another

3. "Uganda: The White Man's Hangover," The World, *Time* 83, no. 1 (January 3, 1964), http://content.time.com/magazine/article/0,9171,940778,00.html.

4. Joseph Conrad and Robert Kimbrough, *Heart of Darkness: An Authoritative Text, Backgrounds and Sources Criticism*, 3rd edition (New York: Norton, 1988), ch. 1, 32–3.

5. Ibid., ch. 1, 10

6. Ibid.

7. Abridged translation without repetitions: Munyau raise the flag. It's three colors. Red is our blood; black is our skin. And green, our land. Raise the flag; raise it high.

8. Norman Maclean Leys, *Kenya*, 4th ed. (London: Frank Cass, 1973), introduction by George Shepperson, 7.

12: Working for the *Nation*

1. African neighborhoods in Nairobi.

2. Now Moi Road, and Sans Chique is gone.

3. See my *Dreams in a Time of War: A Childhood Memoir* (New York: Anchor, 2011).

4. Ibid.

5. See my *In the House of the Interpreter: A Memoir* (New York: Anchor, 2015).

6. Published title of "The Black Messiah."

14: A Hell of Paradise

1. Hugh Dinwiddy, letter to a person he calls "Dear Charles," dated New Year's Day 1997.

2. Isaiah 11:6, 9 (King James Version).

3. Susan N. Kiguli, *Zuhause treibt in der Ferne: Gedichte* [*Home Floats in the Distance: Poems*], in German and English (Heidelberg: Verlag Das Wunderhorn, 2012).

Photograph Sources

Sir Bunsen with the Queen Mother at Makerere graduation, February 20, 1959: courtesy of Makerere University, Makerere University Library–Africana Section

Red-gowned students in front of the Makerere University's Main Building: courtesy of Makerere University

Scene from *Macbeth*: courtesy of Nat Frothingham

Uganda Argus, "A Courageous Macbeth by Makerere Society," November 1961: clipping provided by Nat Frothingham

Penpoint collage by Barbara Caldwell from copies of *Penpoint*: courtesy of Makerere University Library via Mr. Charles Ssekitoleko from the Africana Section of the Main Library

Nyambura, 1960: photo provided by Ngũgĩ's son Kimunya wa Ngũgĩ

Njinjū, Ngũgĩ's younger brother: photo provided by Kimunya wa Ngũgĩ

A collage by Barbara Caldwell of *As I See It* and *Commentary* articles from *Sunday Nation/Daily Nation* written by Ngũgĩ: articles provided by the *Nation* librarian via Peter Kimani

Bethuel Kurutu, Njuguna wa Kimunya, and Ngũgĩ in front of Makerere University's Main Building: from Ngũgĩ's private collection

Actors in *The Black Hermit*. Pat Creole-Rees and John Agard are in the top left corner: from Ngũgĩ's private collection

Actors in *The Black Hermit*. Cecelia Powell, John Agard, and Bethuel Kurutu, in black, are in the middle: from Ngũgĩ's private collection

Scene from *The Black Hermit* with John and Susie: courtesy of Susie Tharu

Ngũgĩ with Hilary Ng'weno: from Ngũgĩ's private collection; photo taken by Bernth Lindfors

Ngũgĩ interviewing Kenyatta and Odinga for the *Nation* at Gatundu: from Ngũgĩ's private collection

Weep Not, Child signing: courtesy of Bernth Lindfors

Poster for *The Black Hermit* by Glen Dias: redrawn from memory

First British edition (1964) of *Weep Not, Child*: courtesy of Wikipedia

Author photo from *Weep Not, Child*: from Ngũgĩ's private collection

Collage by Barbara Caldwell of articles about and by Ngũgĩ in the *Makererean* and *Transition*: articles from the Makerere University Archives with thanks to Mr. Charles Ssekitoleko; *Makererean* and *Black Hermit* articles with thanks to the Africana Section of the Main Library; articles from *Transition* with thanks to Peter Nazareth

The Duke of Edinburgh stands beside Jomo Kenyatta as Kenya regains its "independence" in 1963: image from AFP/Getty Images